PENGUIN BOOKS

WINTER

Karl Ove Knausgaard's first novel, *Out of the World*, was the first ever debut novel to win the Norwegian Critics' Prize and his second, *A Time for Everything*, was widely acclaimed. The *My Struggle* cycle of novels has been heralded as a masterpiece wherever it has appeared, and the first volume was awarded the prestigious Brage Prize.

* * *

Praise for *Winter*

"This lightness of touch may surprise his longtime fans, especially considering the weight of some of the topics he covers. . . . But his ability to weave questions, reflections, and conclusions into such small spaces is often beautiful. . . . When reading these essays, I sometimes paused to ask if Knausgaard was pulling the wool over my eyes with the beauty [of] his prose alone. But no, he doesn't. . . . *Winter* reaches at emotions and common experiences that lay dusty in all of us." —*Chicago Review of Books*

"The author casts the world in a holy glow of surprise and compassion. . . . A winningly interior journey into the most interior of seasons." —*Kirkus Reviews* (starred review)

"One of the most satisfying elements of [Knausgaard's] writing is the rendering of what it is like to be alive, to be a person in the world, whether alone or among people, to walk around as thoughts develop, or to hatch plans with others and participate in activities as a separate being and as part of a whole." —*The Brooklyn Rail*

"I'd have to say that he's awakened a tempest in me. . . . Knausgaard wrote these essays, he said in an interview, 'for fun.' And they are fun . . . and stunning and glorious. . . . It's the seemingly endless stirring of his thoughts about the wide world out there that helps to stir ours." —*The Christian Science Monitor*

"Every child should be as fortunate as Knausgaard's daughter will be some day to have stories like these to usher them into the world." —Bookreporter.com

WINTER
KARL OVE KNAUSGAARD

With illustrations by Lars Lerin

Translated from the Norwegian by Ingvild Burkey

Penguin Books

PENGUIN BOOKS

An imprint of Penguin Random House LLC
penguinrandomhouse.com

Originally published in Norwegian under the title *Om vintern*
by Forlaget Oktober, Oslo, 2015
English-language edition first published in Great Britain by Harvill Secker,
an imprint of Penguin Random House UK, 2017
First published in the United States of America by Penguin Press,
an imprint of Penguin Random House LLC, 2018
Published in Penguin Books 2019

Illustrations by Lars Lerin

Excerpt from "The Gold Rooster" by Olav H. Hauge, translated by Robert Bly.
Reprinted by permission of Robert Bly. From the volume *The Dream We Carry*
by Olav H. Hauge (Copper Canyon Press, 2008).

ISBN 9780399563331 (hardcover)
ISBN 9780399563355 (paperback)
ISBN 9780399563348 (ebook)

Printed in the United States of America
10 9 8 7 6 5 4 3 2 1

Set in Scala

Letter to an Unborn Daughter 1 January

JANUARY

Letter to an Unborn Daughter

2 December. You have lain inside the belly all summer and all autumn. Surrounded by water and darkness, you have grown through the various stages of foetal development, which from the outside resemble the human species' own evolution, from a prehistoric, shrimp-like creature, its spine shaped like a tail and the skin covering the centimetre-long body so thin that its insides show clearly through it – like one of those rain jackets of transparent plastic, which you will see one day and perhaps think, as I do, that there is something obscene about them, maybe because it seems to run counter to nature to see through skin, and that kind of rain jacket is like a skin we put on – to the first mammal-like shape, when the spine is no longer the dominant feature, but rather the head, enormous in contrast to the narrow, curved lower body and the extremely thin, twig-like legs and arms, to say nothing of the fingers and toes, narrow as needles. The facial features are not yet developed – eyes, nose and mouth can barely be discerned – as with a sculpture on which the finer work remains to be done. And that's how it is, I suppose, except that the work isn't done from the outside in, but from the inside out: you change yourself, you emerge through the flesh. This, with vague and indistinct

features, is how you looked at the end of June when we were on holiday on Gotland, in a house that lay deep in the forest on Fårö, in a small clearing among the pines, where the air smelled of salt and the sounds of the sea soughed through the tree trunks. We went swimming before noon, on one of the long, narrow beaches of the Baltic Sea, ate dinner at an outdoor restaurant there, watched movies at the house in the evenings. Your oldest sister was nine years old then, your next-oldest sister was seven, and your brother was five, nearly six. They cause so much fuss, especially the two girls, who are so close in age that they feel they continually need to readjust the distance between themselves, and keep getting into quarrels and sometimes fight, but never when they're at the beach, never when they go swimming; then they're together in everything, and that's how it's always been: in the water all conflicts disappear, all problems, there they forget everything around them and just play. They are also terribly fond of their little brother, they think he's so sweet and sometimes say they would marry him if he wasn't their brother. Two months later he had his first day at school, then it was the end of August, and you were still lying, tiny, in your darkness, your head gigantic compared to your body, your legs like little branches, but with nails on your toes, and on your little fingers, which you were now able to move, and you probably did, putting your thumb in your mouth and sucking it. You had no concept of anything, you didn't know where you were or who you were, but vaguely, very vaguely you must have known that you existed, since there were differences between your various states, for if you didn't feel anything when your hand floated beyond your head, you must have done so when you put it in your mouth, and that difference – that something is something and something else is something else – must be the starting point of consciousness. But it can't have been more than that. All the sounds that made their way in to where you lay, voices and the hum of engines, gulls squawking and music, thuds, rattling, shouts, must simply have been there, like the darkness and the water, something you didn't distinguish as being separate, for there can't have been any difference between you and your surroundings: you were just something that was growing, stretching itself out. You were the darkness, you were the water, you were the bumping when your mother walked down a staircase. You were the warmth, you were the sleep, you were the tiny difference that appeared when you woke up.

One day you will get to see the photographs from your brother's first day at school; one is hanging on the wall in the dining room, the three of them are standing there smiling each in their own typical way, with the garden, green and glimmering in the light of the morning sun, as a backdrop, in their new school clothes, beneath a blue late-summer sky.

This sounds idyllic and joyful. And so it was, both the time spent at the beach on Fårö and the first day of school were good times. But when you read this some day, my little one, if everything goes well and the pregnancy proceeds normally, as I hope and believe it will, but for which there is no guarantee, you will know that that isn't what life is like, that days of sun and laughter are not the rule, even though they too occur. We are at each other's mercy. All our feelings and wishes and desires, our whole individual psychological make-up, with all its curious nooks and corners and its hard carapace, hardened some time in early childhood, almost impossible to crack, confront the feelings and wishes and desires of others and their individual psychological make-up. Even though our bodies are simple and flexible, capable of drinking tea out of the finest and most delicate china, and our manners are good, so that we usually know what is demanded of us in various situations, our souls are like dinosaurs, huge as houses, moving slowly and cumber-somely, but if they get frightened or angry they are deadly, they will stop at nothing to harm or to kill. With this image I mean to say that though everything may seem dependable on the outside, very different things are invariably going on on the inside, and on a very different scale. While on the out-side a word is just a word, which falls to the ground and vanishes, a word can grow into something enormous on the inside, and it can stay there for years. And while an event on the outside is just something that happened, often innocu-ous and soon over and done with, on the inside it can become all-important and generate fear, which inhibits, or create bit-terness, which inhibits, or on the contrary give rise to overconfidence, which doesn't inhibit but may lead to a fall that does. I know people who drink a bottle of strong spirits every day, I know people who pop psychoactive drugs like candy, I know people who have tried to take their own lives – one attempted to hang himself in the attic but was found, another took an overdose in bed and was found and taken to hospital in an ambulance. I know people who have spent long periods of time in psychiatric hospitals. I know people who have been schizophrenic, who have been manic depres-sive, who have had psychoses, and who are totally unable to cope with life. I know people who are bitter and who blame their stagnation or their decline on others, often on account

4

of things that happened ten or twenty or thirty years ago. I know people who abuse their loved ones, and I know people who put up with everything because they expect no more of life.

All this hardening and misery, all this suffering and loss of meaning is also a part of life, and it exists everywhere, but it isn't as easy to see, not just because it originates within but also because most people try to hide it, and because it is so painful to admit: life was supposed to be full of light, life was supposed to be easy, life was supposed to be laughing children running along a beach by the water's edge, who stand smiling into a camera on the first day of school, brimming with expectation and excitement.

Taking one's child to school for the first time, which we will hopefully do with you one day, is a memorable moment for the parents, but also heart-rending, because in there, where they will spend most of their days for the coming fifteen years, they will have to fend for themselves. That is the main thing they are supposed to learn, I think, how to be with others – for the knowledge itself isn't that important, they'll pick that up anyway, sooner or later. A few years ago one of your sisters was going through a difficult time, I saw it but couldn't do anything about it. There were some girls she wanted to be with. Sometimes they played with her, then she was full of joy, sometimes they didn't play with her, then she walked around the school playground by herself, sat alone in the library and read all through the main break. There was nothing I could do. I could talk to her, but first she didn't want to talk about it, and second, what could I say that would help? That she was immensely nice, immensely beautiful, and that all this was just an insignificant episode at the very outset of a life which would unfold richly in ways neither she herself nor we could foresee? It didn't help that I thought she was wonderful if the others didn't. It didn't help that I thought she was funny and smart if they didn't. One evening we were out taking a walk together and she wondered whether we could move somewhere else. I asked where. Australia, she said. I thought, that's as far away as it's possible to get. I asked, why Australia? She said they have school uniforms there. Why do you want a school uniform? I asked. Because then everyone wears the same thing, she said. Why is that important? I asked. Because no one says that my clothes are nice when I have new clothes, she said. They say that to everyone else when they have new clothes. *Aren't* my clothes nice? she said, looking at me. Yes, I said and looked away because my eyes were moist. Your clothes are really very nice.

You will meet with difficulties too. But not for a long time! Now it is December, three months remain until you will be born, and then a few years will follow when you are entirely dependent on us and live in a kind of symbiosis, until that August day arrives when we will send you too to your first day at school. When you read this, that day happened years ago and has become one of your many memories.

Yesterday the temperature dropped sharply, towards evening it was below zero, all the puddles froze, and the car windows were furrowed with frost. Before I went to bed, I stood out in the yard and looked up into the sky, it was completely clear and full of stars. When I came in, Linda was lying on her back in bed with her belly half uncovered. She was just kicking, she said. 'She', that's you. Maybe she'll do it again? I looked at her belly, and then, just a few seconds later, I saw how for a brief moment it bulged, it was as if a little ripple passed over it, almost like the ripples in water when a sea creature moves just beneath the surface. It was your foot, which from the inside kicked up at the ceiling. If you had been born now, you could have survived, though the margins would have been narrow. You dream when you sleep, and you recognise the different sounds you hear.

Maybe you have begun to have an inkling of the outside world, and if you had had the ability to reflect you would probably have assumed that the world consists of a small dark space filled with water, which you are floating in, and that everything beyond it is purely auditive and consists of all kinds of sounds. That this is the universe, and that you are alone in it. And maybe that's how it is out here as well, that we are alone in a large black space filled with stars and planets, and that beyond that space there are sounds, as if from an even bigger space, which we will never be able to penetrate, but only, with time, and perhaps from the very edge of the universe, will be able to hear the sounds of.

It is strange that you exist but you don't know anything about what the world looks like. It's strange that there is a first time to see the sky, a first time to see the sun, a first time to feel the air against one's skin. It's strange that there is a first time to see a face, a tree, a lamp, pyjamas, a shoe. In my life that almost never happens any more. But soon it will. In just a few months I will see you for the first time.

DECEMBER

The Moon

The moon, this enormous rock which from far out there accompanies the earth on its voyage around the sun, is the only celestial body in our immediate vicinity. We see it in the evening and at night, when it reflects the light from the sun, which is hidden from us so that the moon appears fluorescent and seemingly reigns supreme in the sky. At times it appears to be far away, like a small, distant ball, at times it comes closer, and sometimes it hangs suspended like a large luminous disc right above the treetops, like a ship approaching harbour. That its surface is uneven can be seen with the naked eye; some areas are light, others dark. Before the invention of the telescope it was thought that the dark areas were oceans. Others were of the opinion that they were forests. Now we know that the shadows are enormous plains of lava, which at one time pushed up from the moon's interior and filled the craters on its surface before hardening. If one points a telescope towards the moon, one can see that it is completely lifeless and barren and consists of dust and rock, like an enormous sand quarry. Not even a breath of wind ruffles it, ever; the moon is ruled by silence, by immobility, like an eternal image of a world before life, or of a world after life. Is that what dying is like? Is this what awaits us? It probably is. On earth, surrounded by abundant, crawling, flying life, there is something conciliatory about death, as if it too is part of everything that grows and expands, that this is what we disappear into when we die. But that is an illusion, a fantasy, a dream. The interstellar nothing, the absolutely empty and absolutely black, with the eternal and endless solitude this entails, which the moon, since it resembles earth, makes it possible to glimpse briefly, this is what awaits us. The moon is the eye of all that is dead, it hangs there blindly, indifferent to us and to our affairs, those waves of life which rise and subside on earth far down below. But it didn't have to be that way, for the moon is so close that it is possible to travel there from here, as to a distant island. The journey there takes two days. And at one time the moon was much, much closer. Now it is well over three hundred thousand kilometres away from us; when it first appeared, it was only twenty thousand kilometres distant. It must have been gigantic in the sky. Considering the peculiar kinds of creatures which have developed on earth from primordial times until today, with the most remarkable traits to enable them to meet the physical demands of their environment, it wouldn't have taken that much of an adjustment for creatures to appear that were equipped with the qualities required to cross the short distance in space, the way life on earth has always managed to cross the distance to even the most distant islands, and thus has brought life there. The common horsetail, a primitive, primeval plant, couldn't its spools have developed a way of spinning that could have taken them up through the atmosphere and allowed them to drift slowly through space, landing gently in the dust of the moon a few weeks later? Or the jellyfish, couldn't they have left the oceans to float like bells through the air? Air-fish, would that have been any more remarkable than fluorescent, blind deep-sea fish? Not to mention birds. Then life on the moon would have resembled life on earth, but would still have been different, like a radical version of the Galapagos, and the moon's birds, almost weightless, independent of oxygen, would have been able to come in swarms over the earth, visible as tiny specks far, far up there, slowly growing larger, and gliding with their enormous, paper-thin wings over the fields, shimmering in the light of the moon, which for the people of that time was the seat of the sacred and the terrible.

Water

Every day there is water on the table in a big glass jug. It is perfectly clear, perfectly transparent, and has no form of its own: if I pour it into the children's glasses, it at once conforms to the new walls. If I spill it, it flows across the tabletop, faintly bulging, and perhaps it drips down to the floor, for that is the most characteristic property of water, it always seeks the lowest point in space. If it's raining outside, the raindrops glide slowly down the windowpane and onto the ledge, where they gather in clusters, which loosen and fall towards the flagstone below, while the water in the children's glasses, which they lift greedily to their lips, runs down their throats. That this liquid, with no colour of its own, no taste, no form, so easy to control, completely at the mercy of its surroundings, should have anything to do with the waves that every autumn and winter rise out of the ocean along the coast and strike the land with enormous force, this inferno of foam, roaring and booming, is as difficult to grasp as the fact that the tiny flame rising so quietly from the candle wick should have anything to do with the vast fires, many miles across, that occasionally ravage the forests and destroy everything in their path. But it does. Water is on the table, water runs from the tap. Water causes streets to glisten, fields to darken, meadows to glimmer. Water bubbles in brooks, cascades off cliffs, lies still in vast pools in the middle of the forest. Water encircles the continents. In childhood, when the world was still new, it was water we were drawn to. To the pond, to the stream, to the inlet. None of us thought then just what it was about water, but it filled us with something, a suspense, something singular and dramatic, a sort of darkness. Water was an edge, our world ended there, even if it only lay in a pool in the forest a few hundred metres from the lit-up houses, or beneath the concrete bridge down by the small boat marina, where on March evenings we would jump from ice floe to ice floe, strangely elated in the bluish dark, boots and trouser legs heavy with dampness, palms red with cold. More than thirty years later I went back and met my best friend from that time. I asked him if he remembered us jumping on the ice floes. He nodded and was as astonished as I was that we really had, we could easily have died there. And then he told me about something that had happened the year before. He had been walking down that same road, it was winter, late in the evening, it was snowing and visibility was poor, he crossed the bridge, and there, deep down in the black water, he saw light. He leaned over, what the hell could it be, shining down there on the bottom? It was a car that had gone off the road, it must have happened moments ago. He called an ambulance, it arrived, divers made their way down to the wreck, lifted the driver out, he had drowned. The car was hoisted up the next day, and even though I didn't see it myself, I can picture it clearly in my mind, how water gushes from the openings in the suspended body of the car and, splashing, strikes the black surface, on which the whirling snowflakes melt and disappear.

Owls

While the faces of other birds of prey are forward-projecting and in a certain sense aerodynamic, like an extension of the body in flight, with beaks like arrowheads, the owl's face is flat and round, and its beak is small, not unlike a nose. The flat and round character of the face is emphasised by the circle of feathers that surrounds it, and this, that a space seems to have been cleared for the face, rather like a clearing in the woods, makes the owl's face look naked, almost like that of an old man. Presumably this is why in popular belief the owl is viewed as a sinister bird, linked to the powers of the dead: when an owl hoots near the house, someone there will die soon. The other birds of prey are just birds of prey. Though it was said of the eagle that it could carry off small children, and it was considered dangerous, it was never sinister. This was so because the eagle is at one with itself, its shape and its actions form a unified whole, and this unity, however cruel – as when the powerful talons rip open a body and the yellow beak is red with blood and the eyes stare inhumanly straight ahead, soulless and cold – is predictable. The sinister is linked to the unpredictable, the ambivalent, that which veers from one thing to another. The owl is a bird of prey, but its face resembles that of an old man. And although the owl's eyes too have a fixed stare, they are large and round, and besides, owls have eyelids, they blink. I saw an owl once, it was in a wildlife park, and though I wasn't shocked when it suddenly blinked, it was still unsettling. I had never thought of the fact that birds never blink. When this owl, it was an eagle owl, as large as an infant, suddenly blinked, it veered from the bird-like to the human. Together with its perfect calm, this gave the impression that it knew something, that it possessed a form of knowledge, deeper and truer than everything that surrounded us, the asphalted, sunlit walk past the cages, the kiosks selling ice cream and soft drinks and hot dogs, the parents dragging around little carts with backpacks or children in them. This is what has made the owl the companion of Minerva in Roman mythology; she is the goddess of wisdom, music and poetry. When Hegel wrote that the owl of Minerva spreads its wings only with the falling of the dusk, he was thinking of wisdom. This can be taken to mean that wisdom or insight follows the event as night follows day, but it can also be understood as saying that wisdom belongs to the night, the dark, the obscure, the sleeping, that which lies near to the dead yet isn't dead, the borderland where owls roam in popular belief, when with their hoots they warn of the arrival of the dead in the world of the living. And one could certainly say that owls' mythological connection to poetry derives from the same borderland representation. The most striking thing about owls, however, is not what they represent, but what they are, in themselves, as birds. For none of the notions that coalesce around the owl's appearance, the eerie world it appears to glide in and out of, belong to the nature of owls, which is as indifferent and as instinctive as any bird of prey. Owls live by killing small animals, which they rip with their claws and swallow whole. Those parts of the animal that they don't digest, such as bones and skin, they regurgitate in those characteristic balls which one can come across on the forest floor. Everything about owls is geared towards this, even the wreath of feathers around the face, since this wreath captures sounds like a funnel, not unlike the way old-fashioned ear trumpets worked, and since sounds are what owls primarily use to orient themselves when they hunt. Their ears are asymmetrical, which makes them better able to localise the origin of sounds. Owls' night vision is up to a hundred times keener than ours, and their plumage is so extremely soft that their flight is as good as soundless. These characteristics enable them to fly silently through the forest in utter darkness without bumping against tree trunks or branches, and to find their prey on the ground, which receive no warning before the owl's claws sink into them. The owl is nothing other than this: a soundless and highly effective bird of prey. If the true task of poetry is reve- lation, this is what it should reveal, that reality is what it is. That the forest, with its dense spruces and its snow-covered floor, is real. That the falling dusk is real. That the owl taking off from the branch and flying across the field is real. That its soundless wingbeats are real, that the invisible and to us inaudible sound waves that reach its ears are real. That the abrupt change in its flight is real, that the swoop down towards the ground with its claws first is real, that the mouse that the claws dig into is real. That the red of the blood against the grey-white of the mouse's pelt is real as the wings beat and the owl rises through the darkness and in between the tree trunks, which a moment later it vanishes among.

Aquatic Apes

Not much separates human beings from the other mammals, and most of these differences are a matter of degree, language for instance, which in humans has developed into an extremely complex system but which can also be found among apes, cats, dolphins, horses and dogs – even in a creature as far removed from us as the bee – albeit in a radically simplified form. The use of tools too, which human beings have developed so far that they have constructed machines that enter into and replace the work of the body, is also found among other animals, although in infinitely more primitive versions. We have the same needs, for air, water, sunlight and nourishment, we excrete the same waste products through the same body orifices, we have the same basic emotions, hunger, thirst, warmth, cold, the urge to reproduce, and presumably the same supplementary feelings, requiring no action and therefore amounting to a kind of surplus, of satisfaction, joy, sorrow, longing. Whether a bird feels a pang in its chest if it is abandoned we cannot know, but there is no doubt that a dog does. Not even the perhaps greatest difference between humans and other mammals, that the human body unlike that of other mammals has no fur, is absolute, for both the elephant and the rhinoceros have skin instead of fur, and the same goes for nearly all marine mammals, such as dolphins, seals and whales. The question is why just humans, dolphins and elephants are furless, while hardly any other mammals are, not even our closest biological relatives, the apes? In the 1930s the German pathologist Max Westenhöfer advanced a theory that mankind is descended from apes that were forced to abandon a life in the trees. About this there is general agreement, but contrary to the prevailing view within paleoanthropology that these apes lived on the ground in savannah-like surroundings and there developed into humans over the course of hundreds of thousands of years, Westenhöfer believed that the apes were forced even further afield and began to live in water, and that many specifically human traits derive from these hominids' early adaptation to life in the ocean, and remained after they returned to land again. His theory never gained widespread support, and the idea was absent from public life until the 1960s, when independently of Westenhöfer a British marine biologist, Sir Alister Hardy, put forth a similar theory – that apes had developed into semi-aquatic creatures and lived in rivers and beach areas, rather like otters or hippos. Why else would human beings have developed their furless skin, which doesn't provide a single advantage on land? Why else would human infants not learn to walk until they are around one year old, which isn't the case with any other mammal? Why else would the human infant be equipped with a closing reflex, which makes it automatically hold its breath under water? Nor is the movement from land to sea unheard of in evolutionary history – whales are descended from land-living animals related to present-day sheep, goats and deer which gradually began to adapt to a life in water and finally left the land completely, and seals underwent the same development, from land to marine animals, about fifty million years ago. Maybe the hominids, who lived near the water's edge and got nearly all their food from the ocean, the sea or the rivers, unimaginably slowly, the way evolutionary changes occur, increasingly became adapted to an aquatic life. Soon they were spending all their time swimming, diving, splashing, and after a couple of hundred thousand years were hardly recognisable, wholly unlike their close relatives the apes, giving birth to their offspring in water, hairless, some of the males even bald like seals, with protruding noses to protect their respiratory channels against the water, and two long paddling legs with flat, broad feet. It could have gone either way, for if the aquatic apes had done as the whales and seals did and stayed in the water, eventually they would have been able to relinquish their last ties to land and swim out into the oceans, where one might see them today, in pods of hundreds of humanoid marine mammals floating in the water or lying on the rocks, their fingers and toes grown together, hairless, pale, with long, narrow limbs and broad chests for their large lungs, many of them also obese, with enormous rolls of fat, gibbering in their strange, somehow sprawling, almost singing language.

The First Snow

If there are children in the house, the first snowfall is eagerly anticipated. Even here, this far south in Scandinavia, where most winters are entirely or partially without snow, the expectations of snow are strong. The children associate winter, and especially Christmas, with snow, despite the fact that they have experienced a proper snowy winter only once. That the image of winter, from movies and books, overrides reality's rain- and wind-filled days, and seems more real than they do, says a lot about the world of children, which so easily opens itself towards something other than that which exists, and which is so full of hope.

Yesterday, towards late afternoon, the rain turned to snow. Big wet flakes drifted down through the grey sky, filling it with a sudden avalanche of movement, which the children immediately detected. It's snowing! they said and went to stand by the window. The snow didn't stay, but melted as soon as it hit the ground. They went out into the garden and stood there, quietly gazing up into the impenetrable grey, out of which the white flakes were falling, but it was of no use to them, and they soon went back inside. On the flagstone path the snow gradually began to take hold, slowly covering it in a thin shiny-grey layer of slush. In some places, where it lay denser, it was grey-white, in others it had melted into little puddles. On the lawn, which was surprisingly green and eye-catchingly beautiful as it shone amid all the grey, here and there appeared longish shoals of something faintly whitish. Then the temperature must have risen a little, for the snowflakes became greyer and again approached the state of rain, only from the other direction, while at the same time the whitish shadows on the grass became more and more diffuse and finally disappeared completely. As we ate dinner, it was raining outside, and the only thing that brought to mind snow and the hopes of sledding and snow caves connected with it were some grooved, faintly shiny grey stripes which still lay here and there on the flagstones.

In the car this morning, on the way to school through the damp landscape, past the dark brown, nearly black fields and the yellow meadows, I thought that what had happened, of which not a single trace now remained, had been like a manifestation of hesitation itself, of irresolution itself, of vacillation, for there was something deeply familiar about the sequence of events. Winter had almost no self-confidence after the triumph of summer and autumn's resolute clean-up that followed, for what was winter, with its snowfalls and its icing of the waters, other than a cheap conjurer? Turning rain into snow, water into ice, that was all winter was capable of, and that was nothing really, for the change wasn't lasting or substantial and was therefore only apparent. Summer, with all its light and warmth, made plants grow, a recurrent miracle and without doubt of lasting value, for it provided food for animals and humans and thereby maintained life on earth. But snow? And ice? Why, they obstructed life! And though winter might be pretty to look at, and though the children could play in it, it was hard to see any dignity in it. Wasn't winter rather like a tattered, slightly drunken circus ringmaster travelling around with his trailers and campers, providing people with diversion, a few hours when they could gasp in astonishment and shake their heads in admiration, while there really wasn't anything to be astonished at or to admire? On the other hand, thought winter, snowing is the only thing I know. And I do it really well. Why compare myself to summer? We're like day and night, like sun and moon. And if I don't snow, who am I then? Nobody. Then I am nobody. Then that damned self-righteous summer will triumph from here to eternity. Then no one will offer any resistance to that complacent idiot.

So winter decided to snow. Not a little, not hesitantly, not carefully, since it knows that snow is all it has to show for itself, and now it wants to show the world who it is. Winter sets out to fill the whole landscape with snow, to cover it completely, so that everyone forgets summer and begins to think that only winter counts. Oh, they will freeze and skid, they will shovel and plough. Schools will close, cars will get stuck in the ditches, fists will be raised against the sky, cursing winter.

And it starts to snow. But as the sky fills, winter sees how pathetic it is, how little it is, and for a while it tries to compensate by upping the pressure, pouring out still more swirling snowflakes, but it just seems even sillier – what must they think, what kind of vain fool is it who sprinkles a little white powder over the world and thinks that will change anything? For snow *is* nothing. It's *nothing*! And what does that make him if not nobody?

But maybe it isn't too late. If the snow melts as soon as it hits the ground, maybe no one will notice.

And the snow melts as soon as it hits the ground. And the winter turns away in shame. The falling snow turns into rain. Soon every sign of what has just occurred has vanished. For days, even weeks, winter curses itself while it allows autumn to carry on with its middling temperatures, its rain and wind. Then, slowly and imperceptibly, something shifts inside winter, some of the pride in what it is returns, and it begins to miss the action, misses the realisation of its nature, and begins to long for the glittering snow-covered plains, the snowed-in cabins in the woods, the snow banks along the roads. This time winter is calm, not flustered or nearly as fanatical as the last time – what came over it? – and, confident in itself and its powers, it once again lets snow fall, this time upon a frost-covered ground, which doesn't allow a single snowflake to melt and disappear.

Birthday

Every day I get up between four and five to work for a few hours before the others in the house wake up. Today I stayed in bed until seven. I did that because it's my birthday. Not because I wanted to reward myself by sleeping in, but because I didn't want to disappoint the children, who always look forward to the birthday rituals, which consist of them entering the room in single file in the morning, singing the birthday song, carrying lit candles, a tray with breakfast and presents. I lay awake in bed for a while listening to them rustling and bustling down in the kitchen, followed by some intense whispering, before steps sounded on the stairs and the singing began. I closed my eyes and sat up, seemingly muddled with sleep, as they entered. Happy birthday! they said. They watched in excitement as I unwrapped the presents. I had bought them myself the day before in Ystad and given them to Linda in the evening. A pair of leather gloves and a thick brown sweater. What lovely presents! I said. Thank you so much, all of you! That done, they began to lose interest and soon disappeared downstairs again. I dislike eating breakfast in bed, it goes against a strong sense of what belongs where, and as soon as they were out of the room, I got up, dressed and carried the tray down to the kitchen, gobbled down the bread roll standing by the kitchen counter, before

I brought my coffee cup into the dining room and sat down at the table, where they were having breakfast.

To each of them their birthday is one of the greatest events of the year, perhaps the greatest. Nothing makes me happier than that, seeing them bask in the experience of being the centre of attention for a whole day, the feeling it gives them that this day is theirs, their joy over it. My own birthday means nothing any more, except that it gathers time around itself in a very particular way, since it returns every year and in contrast to all the other recurrent dates is singled out. It is as if on that morning I step into a certain room, which I have visited once a year for as long as I can remember. I recognise the variations in the light on that day, the temperature of the air, the various states of the landscape, whether it is raining, snowing, fog or sunshine, and everything wakens memories. Not about events, but about moods. Like now, when the bluish darkness outside the window slowly fades, and I remember what it was like to sit in the classroom on this day and watch the bluish darkness in the school grounds outside fading. Like an old friend of the family who reappears after an absence of many years, the mood from back then strokes my cheek hastily and a little carelessly before it vanishes again.

I have experienced the sixth of December forty-five times. Unless I die in an accident or get seriously ill, I will experience it roughly thirty times more. And it strikes me for the first time that maybe one's lifespan is adapted to one's days, that we die roughly when all the possibilities of variation contained within a given day have been exhausted. When this room consists solely of memories and nothing new can conceivably enter it. That this is what lies in the expression 'sated of days'.

Coins

Coins are small round metal discs, embossed with numbers, letters, patterns and usually a face or a coat of arms. This is how the coin has appeared since time immemorial; a coin minted during the Roman Empire does not differ appreciably from a coin of today. The coin is a means of payment; originally its value lay in the metal, often silver or copper but also gold, while its value now is unrelated to the actual coin, it is an abstraction. This makes the coin a particular variety of fiction. When we read a novel, watch a movie or see a play, what we read or watch is something other than itself, and in order for this representation to be meaningful, we have to believe in it. But our belief does not go beyond the work itself, which forms a separate world in the world, nor is belief absolute, we are always conscious that what we are watching and reading isn't real, even though, to give meaning to it, we pretend that it is. In the case of a coin the fiction is more radical because the belief that it is something else – which isn't absolute either, since we know all along that the coin itself isn't worth anything – has real-world consequences, and these consequences are not fictional but actual occurrences. Our whole society is built around the belief in the fiction of coins, and the moment that belief vanishes, society collapses, as in Germany in the 1930s, when suddenly no one believed that the money was worth anything, as a consequence of which it wasn't.

Coins are generally kept in one's pocket or in one of the closed compartments of one's wallet, but since the value they represent is fairly low, most people have a nonchalant attitude towards them, and might put them, for example, on top of the washing machine or on the shelf beneath the mirror when the pockets are emptied before laundering trousers, and then forget them there, or on the dresser in the hall where keys are usually kept, when the almost truncheon-like weight of them in one's pockets starts to get a little annoying because it keeps pulling one's trousers down a couple of centimetres. And because coins are so small, and fairly heavy relative to their size, they tend to slip out of slanting pockets when one is seated and imperceptibly end up in the depths of the sofa or armchair, or on the floor when one undresses for the night and hangs one's trousers over the back of a chair. So it is no wonder that old coins crop up everywhere on earth where people have settled; they are impossible to keep track of.

For a writer who makes his living by creating fictions, it is strange to see coins lying around in houses and in palms, on shop counters and in cash registers, because they possess such tremendous force, in that they are constantly exchanging their symbolic value for real value, constantly moving in and out between the realm of the imagination and the real world, while at the same time they are so small and negligible. Seen in that light, we are all writers, with money we conjure up a whole society. A particular role is played by the bus driver, who during the 70s walked around with a change dispenser full of coins dangling over his shoulder, heavy and clinking, in which coins lay stacked in metal tubes, five-kroner pieces in one, one-kroner pieces in another, fifty-øre pieces in a third, all connected to a mechanism that released them at the slight push of his thumb, which the driver performed in a practised manner, deftly and familiarly as he walked slowly down the aisle or sat at the wheel with his head turned towards the open door through which new passengers came climbing in, always calm, always confident, this king of fiction, this Homer of coins.

Christina

Christina's face is long and narrow, her skin is pale with freckles, and her hair is brown. Her eyes are also brown. Even though this harmonious colour scale – which ranges from the very sharp, like the chalky white of the eyeballs and the glassy brown of the irises, to the more matt, like the cool white of the skin and the freckles' faded almost beige brown – is genetically conditioned, something she inadvertently possesses or simply is, it still seems typical of her, for the appreciation of colour and form is one of her most characteristic qualities. She is always stylishly dressed, even with limited means, and without spending a lot of time or energy on it. The most prominent part of her face is the area around the mouth, it protrudes slightly, emphasised by the deep furrows that run from the wings of her nose and down past the mouth, not unlike two parentheses, and set it off from her cheeks. The lips are narrow, and often open, so that the teeth are visible between them. This irregularity, that the mouth can only be closed through extra effort and that this has to be remembered, creates a tension in her face, where what usually expresses repose is strained and what appears to be strained is at rest. Her nose is also narrow, and the cheekbones high, with the skin seemingly stretched tight over them. All this gives her face an appearance of sharpness, without ever giving one the impression that this reflects her personality, for there is something mild in her gaze and something soothing in her manner. When she talks to someone, it is rarely about herself, often about them. Consideration characterises what she does, and also who she is: Christina is someone who places others before herself. She is someone who wants others to feel comfortable. But she herself, I often find myself thinking, doesn't seem comfortable. Contentment is rarely among the states her face expresses. Peace of mind is something I have rarely seen in it. Peace of mind comes when there is a balance between the inner and the outer, when the inner flows freely and unhindered into the outer, and vice versa. With Christina it is as if something is always held back, as if something is never let loose, and that energy, of restraint and control, marks her presence, which regardless of how mild and soothing, considerate and self-effacing it is, is always filled too with tension, a stiffness in her face, something thought-out in her movements, as if her soul were forced to fill a form which isn't quite its own, not unlike a state that can be seen in certain horses, where the contrast between the powerful, magnificent body, capable of practically any feat of speed and wildness and daring, and the shy, extremely sensitive and tightly strung spirit, is so great that it seems unreasonable, and one longs on behalf of the animal for it to be spared all these saddles, halters, boxes and stables, all these elaborate exercises and performances, and just be allowed to gallop on a plain, free from everything, including itself.

Chairs

A chair is for sitting on. It consists of four legs upon which rests a board, and from the end of this rises a backrest. All these elements can be executed in various ways, shaped differently and using different materials, but the basic shape is fixed and unalterable: if one of the elements is missing, such as the backrest, it is no longer a chair, but something else, in this case a stool. The chair is related to the bench and the sofa, which are also for sitting on, yet is still radically separate from them, for the chair is for one person, and one person only, which is an essential aspect of its character. The chair isolates us, it is like a little island in the room, to which no one else has access as long as someone is in possession of it. In other words, the chair always has an element of reserve about it, even though in principle it is open to anyone. This form, something at once open and reserved, is found everywhere in society, where for every vacant position there are always plenty of candidates, who are all in principle eligible, yet it invariably ends up being given to only one of them. The game of musical chairs, which is played at so many children's parties, is in that sense a realistic exercise in the weeding-out practised by society that awaits the children. To play the game, a certain number of chairs are set in a circle, always one fewer than the number of children who are walking around them, while music is played. When the music stops, the children sit down on the chairs, all except the one child who can't find one. That child is then out of the game, which continues after one more chair has been removed from the circle, so that the children who start walking around again are always one too many. The game ends when the last child is seated on the last remaining chair, like a king on his throne. The chair's autarchic character is so well established that it is unthinkable that two adults should share a chair, whether through sitting next to each other, or one of them sitting on the other's lap. Children may do that, but not adults. Even a couple would cause some discomfort if they did that in front of others, while they might easily have sat closely entwined on a sofa or a bench.

The chair is a symbol of power, the king has his throne, the chieftain has his chair, the minister has his seat in the government. But the chair is also something everyone has at home and which everyone, infants as well as the very old, sits on every day. And like everything that the body uses regularly, from stairs to door handles, water taps and coffee cups to tables and remote controls, soap dispensers and clothes hangers, the particular chair, with its particular appearance, is lost sight of – when we enter a room with chairs in it, we know they are there, without this certainty usually reaching our consciousness and becoming a clearly formulated thought. It is as if we live in a world of shadows. This is what Ingmar Bergman draws on when in the film *Fanny and Alexander* he lets the father, outstandingly acted by Allan Edwall, spellbind the children in the nursery on Christmas Eve by pulling out a chair. You think this is a regular nursery chair? he says and pauses. But it isn't, he continues. And then he tells them the fantastic history of the chair. Once it belonged to the empress of China, he says, and the children stare at him with open mouths and sparkling eyes. When the father finishes his tale and replaces the chair against the wall, the chair is no longer the same, and in the eyes of these children it has changed for ever, the viewer realises. Never again will that chair be just a chair. It is a beautiful scene, but also sentimental, and it is difficult to accept its moral, at least for me, for the chair is really just a chair; what causes it to glow, there in the darkness of the nursery, isn't actually true, it doesn't really belong to the chair, has nothing to do with it really, it's just a fairy tale. The scene is deeply alien to everything Ingmar Bergman had hitherto represented in his films, where he constantly sought to deprive the world of its illusions, to see through them and create images of the world as it really is. Perhaps *Fanny and Alexander* is best understood as a fable in which battle is waged between two forces, those that add to and those that subtract, and Bergman saw himself as one who added to reality, based on the certitude that the act of creating, realistic or not, minimalistic or not, is always, regardless, adding something which wasn't there before. And for the children in the nursery, the chair will not shine in their recollection primarily because of the stories their father told about it, but because it was their father who told them, for not long after this scene he dies, and it will be the person he was, one might imagine, that they will remember every time they see the chair, that he was one of the rare people who opened out the world instead of closing it.

Safety Reflector

For animals a key survival skill has always been to merge as much as possible with the darkness at night. During the day, when they can see whatever is moving in their surroundings and take it into consideration, some of them can be strikingly flamboyant and loud, but at night what counts is immobility, invisibility and silence. All life is in one way or another geared towards that requirement. This is how it's been on earth for millions of years. From that perspective, the danger that the car and the train represent is so new that it still hasn't impressed itself on the behavioural pattern of animals. In landscapes crossed by roads and railway lines, not being seen at night may entail sudden and violent death. When I drive from here into Malmö in the morning, there are often dead animals lying in the road, mostly hedgehogs and badgers and cats, but also the occasional fox. I feel a pang in my heart at the sight, but that little grief is something I can't afford to indulge in; soon enough I am thinking of something else. Before I got my driving licence, I didn't realise how difficult it is to see figures on the road in the dark. That a person who isn't wearing a safety reflector is to all intents and purposes invisible. All campaigns promoting the use of reflectors, which I used to think were exaggerated, part of a spreading culture of safety which obstructed children's natural development and made everything seem a risk, I now sympathise with entirely. And I always keep close to the centre line when I drive in the dark. I did that yesterday too. Around ten in the evening we were on our way home from Simrishamn, where one of our daughters had been performing in a Christmas play and the rest of the family had been there to watch her. We were six people in the car, the darkness was dense, even though the sky was starlit, and I drove fast, since I know this road like the back of my hand. Wide fields on both sides, completely concealed by the dark except where the lights from the farms opened it up. Long, perfectly straight stretches where I could do a hundred, a hundred and ten kilometres an hour, interrupted by small villages where the speed limit was fifty. After passing through Hammenhög we were on our way across the plain. Suddenly a roe deer came running into the beam of the headlights. I hit the brakes and just barely managed to steer clear of it, but not the next one. The car caught its hindquarters. It was flung around with indescribable brutality. The encounter with the car tore it out of its path and into another, twisted and crippled, with its hind legs in the air, its front legs and head pressed against the asphalt, and the next moment it was out of sight. I stopped the car in a lay-by just beyond, walked back along the road, couldn't at first see the animal. Could it have survived? Could it have just kept running? Then I noticed a contour which stood out from the ground, and after staring at it for a few seconds, I realised it was the deer. It lay as if resting, and it was alive, for its head was lifted and it was trembling slightly. I took out my mobile phone and dialled the police. The little screen shone intensely in the dark. I said my name while I looked at the trembling dark grey outline in the ditch, before it became unbearable and I lifted my gaze to the sky, which was full of sparkling stars.

Pipes

Pipes transport flowing liquids. Pipes come in all sizes and in all materials, from gigantic concrete pipes that transport lake water down to power station turbines to the smallest capillaries, thin as strands of hair, that lead blood from one place in the body to another. Characteristic of pipes is that they are round, they are hollow and they are open at both ends. With its firm walls the pipe gives form to what is liquid, gathers and concentrates it, so that it cannot adhere to the law which generally applies to liquids – to spread out, sink down, percolate, dissipate. The pipe is related to the gutter, which is a kind of open pipe, where whatever is flowing is visible, and with the cable, which is a kind of pipe without a hollow centre, where something that isn't liquid, but which isn't solid either and can hardly be said to have physical extension but still moves, like electricity, is led from one point to another. Together these three, the pipe, the gutter and the cable, connect all our buildings and form a vast physical network which lies coiled, serpent-like, around the globe, both above and below ground. In this way they ensure our freedom: we can be self-sufficient in our houses and don't need to spend time and effort to get hold of what we need, whether it is water to wash our hands, or the daily news, or to transport out what we have used, like excrement or bath water. On the other hand, they expose our dependency, for what is the pipe that leads to the water tap other than an extension of the gullet, the pipe that leads out from the toilet bowl an extension of the colon and the urethra, the cable that transports images to the TV an extension of the eyes, and the cable that transports information to the computer an extension of the brain? We live within this web of pipes and cables, and whether we are free depends on whether in this web we are like the spider or rather like the spider's prey. I would say both, we are now one and now the other, and this alternation is a fundamental trait of our being, going back to the time we spend in our mother's belly, connected to her via the umbilical cord, which is a cross between a pipe and a cable, through which flows everything we need to exist. It is cut off when we are born, but the dependency it represents is continued in other ways, first to our mother, when we are breastfed by her and the milk flows from inside her through countless little tubes and into us, and then to the people around us through the system of pipes and cables which, like the great Midgardsorm serpent of Norse mythology, lies coiled around the earth and which we spend the rest of our lives connecting to and disconnecting from. That our body is filled with liquids, and that our life depends on the distribution of these liquids from one organ to the other, through thousands of little pipes which vary in size from the tube-like intestines to the capillaries of the brain, and that all life, even the most primitive of trees, is coursed through by pipes in this manner, makes the principle of the pipe perhaps the most important of life's requirements, and humankind akin to the reed.

Mess

We are one of those families whose homes are messy. That this bothers me, not intensely but steadily and quietly, is clear from the way I formulate it – that we are one of a number of families to whom this applies is obviously a way to render the mess harmless, to spread it out among more people and thus to lessen it. We're not the only ones whose house is messy, we belong to a larger group of people, so being messy is a common human condition and nothing to be ashamed of. But that's exactly how I feel. When there is a knock on the door and I open it so that the visitor can look into the hall, where the shoes and boots are not lined up against the wall or ranged neatly on the shoe rack, but lie scattered all over the floor, and the bench beneath the window is covered with all kinds of clothing, even towels which the children have left there on their way from the bathroom to the living room, and from the wall below the staircase rises a small mountain of roller skates, bicycle helmets, riding helmets, riding breeches, gym bags, backpacks, and strewn about amid all this there are leaves, twigs, blades of grass, clods of soil and pebbles, in addition to caps and mittens, scarves and socks, I feel ashamed and want only for the visitor to leave, so that this shame, which flaps around in me like one of those large

49

hollow figures through which air is blown and which sometimes flutter about outside shopping centres or fast-food restaurants, can die down. But the people who come here are usually the parents of our children's friends, who are either picking up or dropping off their own children, and then it seems natural to invite them in, at least into the hall, while their child takes off or puts on their outer clothing. At such times, when they see how messy our house is, I always think this is the last time they'll visit. Sometimes when they are standing there in the hall waiting, the children are upstairs, and sometimes it happens that they refuse to come down, and since I can't persuade other people's recalcitrant children the way I can my own, by coaxing and cajoling, reasoning, making offers and threatening, the mother or father has to go upstairs themselves, where the mess is even greater. It's terrible. But everyone pretends not to notice, even though the mess that surrounds us is obviously on their minds too. It has never happened that a visitor has said, I'll say, your place is certainly a mess! I've never seen anything like it! And do you like it this way? You should clean the place up! We'll be keeping our Tilda away from here until you clean up your act. If you're able to, that is?

The mess in our house seems to adhere to certain laws, it collects in particular places. On the kitchen counter, under the cupboards where the cups and glasses are kept, where we usually put the mail, an enormous pile always springs up, not just envelopes and advertising, newspapers and parcels, but also books, toys, bags, plastic boxes, socks, pens and felt-tip markers, hairbands, tools, screws and nails, fuses and light bulbs. This pile grows slowly and follows a very different rhythm to the pile on the opposite counter, by the sink, where a mountain of dirty dishes abruptly rears up, on good days disappearing again after only a couple of hours, while on bad days it continues to grow there too. Upstairs the mess is static, it consists mainly of toys and arches up from the walls towards the centre of the rooms, where a fairly narrow path is kept open. On the whole, the way our mess spreads out is not unlike the way snow distributes itself in the forest, in some places piling up against tree trunks, in others lying in deep drifts, and in others again spreading out in rather thin layers. But mess is not a meaningful concept when applied to nature, regardless of how wildly a thicket grows or how many trees a storm has toppled or a forest fire has charred, and this is so because nature doesn't have two levels, one ideal and one real, but only exists on one level, the level of the real. A household or a family, on the other hand, exists in the real and aspires towards the ideal. All tragedies arise out of this duality, but also all triumphs. And the feeling of triumph is what prevails in me now, when the kitchen in the house on the other side of the lawn, lit up like a train compartment in the darkness, where only a few hours ago I did the Christmas cleaning, is sparkling clean and bright.

Winter Sounds

Walking in the forest in winter is quite different from walking there in summer. By autumn the forest is already emptying of sound, as the migratory birds fly south, and the leaves on the trees, which all through the summer half of the year have filled the woods with their rustling and murmuring, drop off. When the cold comes the brooks freeze over, and their constant purling and babbling – which if they are large enough sounds from a distance like rushing wind or even, if the streaming water resonates from clefts or steep hillsides, like a roar – cease. The first covering of snow causes the last sounds, of feet rustling through dead leaves, to disappear, at the same time as other, heavier treads are muffled. In the following months, it is this silence that reigns. But just as a hitherto drab and anonymous colour can suddenly blaze against the white, if it stands alone, it is as if the few and sporadic sounds that remain in the forest grow in strength and intensity against a backdrop of silence. The screech of a crow, for instance, which in summer is just one note in a greater tapestry of sound, in winter is allowed to fill the air alone, and every single nuance in its rasping, hoarse, seemingly consonant-filled caws stands out: how they rise aggressively at first, then descend mournfully towards the end, leaving behind a sometimes melancholy, sometimes eerie mood among the trees. Just as striking is how loud the sounds of one's own movements become, it is as if the entire forest were filled with the faintly sandpapery noise of synthetic surfaces being rubbed and chafed against each other, until one stops and the sounds stop too, and it falls silent the way it does when a droning engine one has become used to and no longer notices is abruptly switched off. Only one's breathing continues to be audible, like a faint hissing from a valve, rising and falling, as if expelled by the plunging of a piston, which both the throbbing in the temples and neck and the wisps of smoke escaping from one's mouth seem to be connected with. It is impossible to have such thoughts in summer, when we are more at one with our movements and sounds. But winter not only muffles some sounds and intensifies others, it also has sounds that are entirely its own, unique to the season, and some of them are among the most beautiful of all. The low boom of ice-covered waters as they freeze, for instance, which can be heard on perfectly clear days or nights when the cold deepens, and which has something menacing or mighty about it, since it isn't connected to any visible movement. Just the motionless, steely surface, the jagged black spruces surrounding it, the sparkling stars in the darkness above, the booming from the ice below. But the winter's song of songs, that is the razor-sharp, criss-crossing sound of speed skates as the blades cut across the ice and leave it. The still sharp but slightly more blunted knocking of hockey skates, which turns into a brief sizzle when the skater whirls abruptly and the blade works counter to rather than gliding along the ice, as a shower of fine-cut surface ice is flung away from it, is not as grand but still captivating. Not to mention the soft muffled thud of broad slalom skis hitting the ground in parallel after sailing through the air, muted by new snow so that the sound is almost a *poof,* but not quite; *tomp* is what it sounds like. All these sounds are characteristic of winter, since they are heard only then, yet they can't be said to express winter, only aspects of it. White is the absence of colour, so the equivalent of whiteness in the world of sound must be silence. When the snow-covered forest lies motionless beneath the faintly darkening sky, it is completely still. If it then begins to snow and the air fills with snowflakes, it is still completely silent, but the silence is different, it seems to grow denser, more concentrated, and that sound, which is no sound, only a nuance of silence, a kind of intensifying or deepening of it, is the sonic expression of winter's essence.

Christmas Presents

It's the night before Christmas Eve. Earlier today I was out shopping, first for groceries, six shopping bags full of wrapped and glistening Christmas foods, fruit, nuts, soft drinks and beer, then I stopped at a toyshop and a bookshop to buy the last presents for the children. The sky was grey and heavy, and though it wasn't raining the landscape seemed saturated with moisture, the way it always is here in the winter: wet, dark soil, shimmering grass, naked trees, a persistent wind. Now I am sitting in my office, surrounded by wrapping paper, rolls of tape, sheets of stickers, many-coloured ribbons and two piles of presents, one of those that are already wrapped, one of those that still need wrapping. The only light comes from a floor lamp next to the desk, it lights up the floor beneath it in a circle, which grows fainter and fainter and in the corners of the room is nearly gone. It gives me the feeling of being in a grotto. Just a few minutes ago, as I sat on the floor cutting paper, placing presents on top, wrapping them, taping and winding ribbons around them, I was connected to all of these things, there was hardly any difference between them and me, we were part of the same whirl of movement. Now I see them as isolated objects from different parts of the world that have accidentally ended up here, with no other connection to the living than the one in my mind. The robot, for instance, lying propped up against an unopened roll of wrapping paper, maybe thirty centimetres long, grey and made of plastic, is just a thing, it is closed like a rock on a beach. Not to mention the stuffed rabbit lying on its back on top of a plastic bag a bit further away. They neither give nor take anything, they are just here, the way logs, leaves, branches, pine needles and various small plastic objects just pile up in a backwater in autumn. But tomorrow evening, when the children unwrap them, they will be given names and traits and be included as equal members of their world. This ability, to give life to the lifeless, to create a world where that which is closed opens itself to us, is ennobled in literature, for in principle there is no difference between what happens when I open one of the books here, say Tolstoy's *War and Peace*, and when the children unwrap their presents tomorrow. A little ink on a page wakens a tempest of emotions and causes everything else to vanish, as also happens when the robot takes a few steps across the floor or the rabbit is pressed close and ardently kissed. The bridge between those two dead worlds, that of literature and that of toys, is perhaps the wish list, which has none of the toys' tangibility but only invokes it the way literature has always invoked the tangible world and set it tumbling around weightlessly in our minds. But in contrast to literature, wish lists can be converted into goods, and that's why I sit here every year; amid this river of presents I am attempting to realise their dreams. They themselves think that Christmas presents are only about this, but I know that the gifts have a longer journey to travel: like hope, they come sailing from the islands of the imaginary future and onto reality's shores, where they gain weight and presence, but not for long, for they are travelling on, out on the other side, into the lost past, where their lives will continue as incorporeal memories, which is perhaps the most important part of their existence, preserving the memory of the Christmases of childhood.

Father Christmas

Yesterday evening I was standing on a gravel road, it was drizzling, I was dressed in a red coat, on my feet I wore long woollen stockings over my best shoes, and on my head I wore a mask which seemed to stare up into the damp and compact darkness of the sky. In one hand I held a jute sack, in the other an old-fashioned lantern. As I approached the lit-up house at the end of the road, I stopped, opened the lantern, lit the tea light, closed the little hatch, pulled the mask down over my face, slung the sack over my shoulder, bent my back and walked with the short steps of an old man over to the window. Up until now I had felt a little nervous, but the nervousness disappeared the moment I bent over, it was as if I had become an old man and was no longer playing the part. I rapped on the window. There was the sound of running steps from within, and I drew back a little. A child's face was pressed against the windowpane. I lifted my hand in trembling greeting and continued over to the entrance door, which shortly after was flung open. Merry Christmas to all, I said in a piping voice. The boy stared at me intensely for a few seconds, clearly prepared to expose me, before he rather anxiously withdrew. His parents appeared, they looked smilingly at me and asked whether I wanted something to fortify myself. I shook my head. I'm driving, I said, looking at the boy. What is your name, then? I asked. He said his name. I repeated it, mumbling to myself as I rummaged through the sack. When I handed him his present, he tore off the wrapping in an explosion of movement. Shortly after I was standing outside again, by the short wall of the house, with the mask pulled up over my head and a glowing cigarette in my mouth. The father came out, peering around him. Over here! I said in a low voice. Well, that went pretty well, he said, stopping in front of me. Yes, I said. It seems he fell for it this year too. Can I bum one off you? the father asked. Sure, I said. We walked along the road to my car, which was parked at the end of it, at the crossroads where the main road went by. We got in. Smart move to park here, the father said. He was sure he was going to find you out because of the car. Yes, I said, and drove into the countryside. The road was completely deserted, even as it passed through the village, there wasn't a person in sight. I parked near the school, and we got out into the rain. Would you like a whisky? I asked. He nodded, and I got out the glasses and the bottle I had in the car, poured us drinks. It was unusually quiet; on any other evening a car would have passed occasionally. When our glasses were empty, I put mine back in the car, took off my coat and handed it to him. He stuck one arm into the sleeve, took the whisky glass in his other hand and stuck his other arm in. The coat-tails flapped in the wind. I handed him the mask. So you'll be along in a couple of minutes then, I said and started towards the house. Two of the children came out when they heard the door open. They had refused to believe that I had really gone out to buy cigarettes, so I held the packet out to them as proof. I'm not

Father Christmas, and I've been to the petrol station to buy cigarettes, just like I said, I said. They didn't know quite what to believe. Just then there was a knock on the door. Who can it be? I said. The older child gave me an ironic look. I opened the door, and there was Father Christmas with the lantern in his hand and the sack over his shoulder. Are there any good children here? he said. He didn't have a piping voice, but spoke with a Finland-Swedish accent. Mum, Mum, Father Christmas is here! the youngest shouted. The others at the party came out, and the hall filled with people, we stood in a semicircle staring at Father Christmas, who rummaged slowly through his sack and pulled out presents one by one, handing them solemnly to the children, who stared at him as if in a daze. Would you like something to fortify yourself? I asked, and he nodded, downing the glass of cognac in one go.

After he left, the children were far too engrossed in the presents to notice that I went out after him. He was standing by the car waiting for me, still wearing the mask.

It struck me how sinister he looked, in those familiar surroundings, with the grotesque mask covering his face.

I took out the bottle again and poured two drinks, handing him one.

Well, merry Christmas, he said, raising his glass.

Merry Christmas, I said.

Guests

Home is the place where, when you have to go there, they have to take you in, the saying goes. It is also the place where you don't act a part but are yourself. If you have to act a part, if you have to pretend, you are a guest in your own home. Guests are people staying temporarily in a place where they don't belong. It could be at a hotel, where one pays to stay, or it could be with other people, usually relatives or friends, in their home, where no pecuniary consideration is expected. This creates an imbalance in the relationship which resembles that introduced by a gift: the guests receive, the hosts give. Therefore it is incumbent upon the guests to show gratitude, that they appreciate the gift, and they do this by praising it, by saying how beautiful the hosts' home is, by offering to help and generally trying to impose as little as possible. A good host declines all offers of help and tries to satisfy the guests' every need, preferably well before the need arises. This formal game maintains their respective roles, the distance between them, and though the roles are at odds with each other – the host who makes plenty of room for the guests, the guests who try to take up as little space as possible – precisely because it is a game it is easy to relate to, each side being visible at all times: as long as one sticks to the roles and doesn't exceed them, nothing is hidden and no conflict is possible. The moment there is a deviation from expected roles, if the host sets the table with an audible sigh, for instance, thereby giving the guests to understand that she has other and better things to do, or the guests sit down at the breakfast table without praising it or in other ways acknowledging the efforts of the host, but simply take them for granted, and maybe even say that they prefer their bacon crispy not soft, and give the host advice on how to make it crispy, namely by placing it in a preheated frying pan and not heating it slowly with the pan as she has obviously done with these soggy, grease-drenched strips, then the clear-cut boundaries between guest and host are erased, an ambiguity arises, and in interpersonal relations frustration and suspicion feed off ambiguity and are strengthened by it. Therefore it is easier to have friends as guests, or to be the guest of one's friends, than it is to have family as guests. Family ties are strong, much stronger than the temporary bonds established by the roles of guest and host. If the host's mother comes to visit, for instance, it will often be difficult for her not to behave as a mother in her son or daughter's house too, since that is what she is permanently in her own mind, and even if she doesn't take charge of everything, cooking meals, standing in the kitchen frying and broiling, cleaning the cupboards or folding the clothing in the chests of drawers, her presence will still challenge the distinction between host and guest by dissolving the notion of home and belonging simply by virtue of her being there: home is where she is. This turns the home all at once into a role, or at least into a secondary home, an attempt to imitate or create an alternative to the primary home. What happens then is that everything that isn't working in the home, everything that isn't as it should be, suddenly becomes visible, for another of the functions of the role is that it only relates to appearances, so that a dissolution of the role also entails a dissolution of appearances, revealing the real state of affairs. In a home the real can be tolerated, that is a part of its function, since a home and all things domestic are not intended for other people, but conform to the standards, requirements and possibilities of the people living there. In a home that is spotlessly maintained, always sparkling clean and perfectly orderly, the presence of a parent can bring to light something neurotic, an unhealthy obsession with what others might think and believe, a life where appearances are more important than reality, while a parental presence in a home that is messy, dirty and disorderly can expose shiftlessness, passivity, spinelessness, weakness.

In the five years we have lived here we have hosted the whole spectrum of guests, from the most considerate and solicitous to those who have come barging in and taken over our home with their presence, those oblivious guests who treat others' homes like their own, thereby turning us who live here into guests. Few things infuriate me more than that, but I refuse to relinquish my role as host, so I pick up after them with a smile, I even nodded pleasantly and as if in agreement when the guest during a shopping trip yesterday removed some pieces of meat from my basket and said that we couldn't eat such expensive cuts, it was unethical and immoral, and when later the same evening I was frying the cheap cutlets on the kitchen stove I didn't protest when he grabbed my spatula and turned the cutlets over in the frying pan, but stepped politely aside. After we had eaten and were sitting around the table, with the winter darkness like a black sea outside the windows, I also abstained from following the urge to go into my office, fetch *The Poetic Edda* and read aloud to them from 'Hovamal', this Norse exposition of the ethics of guesthood, where in verse thirty-five it is said:

> *Forth shall one go,*
> *nor stay as a guest*
> *in a single spot for ever;*
> *Love becomes loathing*
> *if long one sits*
> *by the hearth in another's home.*

The Nose

The nose is a dramatically sloping and conspicuous growth that protrudes from the middle of the face beneath the eyes and above the mouth, with which it is also connected via interior channels. The old notion about the first human having been moulded out of clay may well have originated from observing the nose, which not only has an air of something constructed about it – the bones like stays over which the cartilage and the skin are stretched like a small tent – but also something modelled, for in the area between the nasal bone and the wing of the nose there is a small dent, which it is easy to think of as having been formed by a finger which has carefully been adding matter and then shaping the wing of the nose by rubbing it out, layer after layer, pushing it in a little near the bone to give it the right curve, and in this way leaving a dent. Perhaps the most striking thing about the nose, however, is that it ends so abruptly, in two arched portals – which give the nose a vague resemblance to a church – and that these portals, separated from each other by the septum, always remain open. All the other body orifices can be closed, either by sphincter muscles, as in the rectum or the mouth, or with folds of skin, like the labia and the foreskin, or by a permanent inner wall, as in the ears.

Only the nostrils always remain open. This is clearly because it is through them that the greater part of the air we breathe flows in. A gate here, which could go up and down, as in a garage, for instance, or some more hatch-like contraption, like the one many cat owners have in their outside doors, would have been extremely cumbersome and unnecessarily energy-consuming and would also have entailed a certain risk, for it doesn't take more than a few minutes' interruption to the air supply before we die, and even though the mouth is there partly as a back-up for the nose, in that they share the channels that lead both up into the head and down into the lungs, an unobstructed opening through the nose is probably the best solution anyway.

With this in mind, one would think that the nose, this tent pitched on our cheeks, this church of our visage, would be the central feature and most important part of the face – the nose is the only part of the face that stands out, it is located at the very centre of it, and through its long construction, similar to the side aisle of a cathedral, flows the only thing we need a constant supply of to stay alive. So shouldn't it be the nose that we address when we meet another human being? Shouldn't the nose be the key to identifying this person's character, personality, type, soul?

But it isn't. That privilege has been awarded to the eyes.

That precisely the eyes have come to symbolise the inner person to the outside world isn't so strange, for in contrast to the nose, the eyes are mobile, they can move to either side and up and down, and thus are better suited to representing a person's inner self, which is always mobile and fluid, regardless of how stiff and rigid someone may seem to others. But more important is the fact that the eyes are the only place on the body's exterior that isn't covered by skin (with the exception of the nails and hair, but they are dead), thereby giving the impression that one can look in through them, not unlike the windows of a house. Perhaps it also counts for something that the eyes have been provided with two garage-like gates which the nose has been denied, namely the eyelids, which can be opened and closed at will, projecting flexibility and again emphasising the static character of the nose. And with regard to the soul it is also the case that vision, the sense possessed by the eyes, takes precedence over smell, the sense belonging to the nose, for the simple reason that the one who is seen also sees the one they are seen by, thereby revealing much of their inner self. It is also significant that the eyes don't age – in contrast to the nose, which in old age becomes both longer and redder, and in the elderly can resemble a caved-in barn – since the soul doesn't age either, but remains the same throughout our lives. That the waste product of the eyes is tears, exalted in songs and poems, while the waste products of the nose are snot and blood doesn't improve matters for the nose. Moreover a beautiful nose is a nose which isn't noticeable, a nose which is so symmetrical, tidy and narrow it doesn't deflect attention from any of the face's other features. A particularly long, broad, flat or crooked nose is a disaster for a face, and demands a great deal of its possessor, since from an early age it must be obvious that what people associate with that person is their remarkable nose, and this has to be borne somehow, in a protracted inner struggle over identity, lasting at least throughout their teens, before they can reconcile themselves to it. I saw a nose like that once, it was in the early 1990s, I was in Prague with Espen, and we were in a small grocery shop when he tugged at me and said in a low, eager voice, Did you see him? Who? I said. The guy with the nose, Espen said. Over there. I looked. And I couldn't believe what I was seeing. A dark-haired, bashful, rather thin fellow, maybe in his forties, was standing there with an enormous nose planted in the middle of his face. It was long as a handle, and knobbly as if full of little protuberances. It looked like a root. It is the most shocking thing I have ever seen. Impossible to take one's eyes off. He looked like the old woman in the fairy tale, the one who got her nose stuck in the chopping block, or like a caricature from the Middle Ages, when the grotesque was a conspicuous feature of human beings. Both Espen and I forgot everything we knew about manners and stood there staring at him for what must have been several seconds. He noticed, obviously, and turned away. What was it that fascinated us so? With a nose that long, it was as if he was no longer human but something else. Something bestial, some thing growing uncontrollably, which could have been the Devil or Pan, if not for the fact that his attribute, the nose, was also comical, and has been considered so for thousands of years. We went out, positioning ourselves on the other side of the road, and when he came out and started walking away, we followed him. That's how powerful the pull exerted by his nose was. But now, more than anything it is his gaze I remember, when he realised that we were staring at him, that brief glimpse of something extremely pained which appeared in his eyes and was the very opposite of the bestial nose, yet produced by it, and which I now think of as almost the quintessence of the human condition.

Stuffed Animals

Up on the first floor, where the children lie asleep in three beds fixed to the floor in a row, as if on board a ship, there are lots of stuffed animals, maybe as many as a hundred. There are polar bears, brown bears, raccoons, wolves, lynxes, dogs and cats. There are cows, horses, sheep, hedgehogs, rabbits, crows and owls. There are lions, tigers, crocodiles, giraffes, seals, whales, sharks and dolphins. They have been made with a certain realism and have kept some of their character-istic traits – the seals have flippers, the elephants have trunks, the crows have beaks – but have been drawn, as it were, within the children's horizon, so that they are all more or less the same size, soft and made of cloth, they can be held in one's arms and hugged, dispossessed of their hard parts, everything that can bite, strike, peck, claw. The chil-dren have held them close in bed in their sleep, carried them around with them on their travels, played with them on rainy days. That doesn't mean that they are ignorant about the natural lives of these animals – all of them have been highly interested in the bloodthirstiness of sharks, for instance, and have viewed a number of video clips of shark attacks on YouTube – but they have chosen to disregard all aggression and violence when it comes to their stuffed animals, which for them belong to a separate universe, disconnected from external reality, with only the body shapes intact. The wolf lies beside the lamb, the lion beside the zebra. The stuffed animals act as agents for their feelings, an extension of their inner world, and the striking thing is how strong their wish is for everyone to be kind and to live for ever. But when the realities of the world hit them, for instance when they begin to ride horses and grapple with the huge animals in the stable, with their hard hooves and teeth, their massive flanks and large, nervously jerking heads, so difficult to put a halter on, or when the cat comes along with a bird dangling from its mouth, which it triumphantly drops on the doorstep, and the bird half flaps its wings in an attempt to escape its fate, and the cat playfully flings its paw out after the feather-clad little body, or crunches into it with its teeth, it doesn't mean that the stuffed animals' separate reality is shattered, that they transfer their experiences of the world onto them – no, up in their room everything is sheer softness and goodness, there sharks are sleeping companions and lions are cuddled. I don't think the stuffed animals are a flight from reality, a bulwark against brutality and everything hard, that they represent the world as they wish it were, it is rather that the stuffed animals represent them, that this is what their souls look like, small, soft, good and faithful. Even for a time after they have put aside their stuffed animals, when they lie abandoned and scruffy up in the attic, maybe crammed into a cardboard box with their eyes permanently open, the children will react instinctively against the suffering brought on by war and the destitution of poverty, demand justice and equality in the naivety of early adolescence, which is the final phase of the child soul, when for the first time it stands open to the world beyond in a battle it can never win, since by nature it is defenceless and can therefore only live on within them as something else, harder and tougher in those that survive, thin and glass-like in those whom the world will crush.

Cold

It is cold out these days. We have underfloor heating cables in the house, but they don't work. Only the living room and the bedrooms are electrically heated, while the kitchen, the bathroom, the corridors and the dining room are ice-cold when we wake up. More often than not I lie beneath the covers dreading the thought of getting up, mustering my courage before I go down the cold stairs, across the cold tiles in the hall and onto the cold wooden floor in the kitchen. The body seems to contract, as if trying to minimise the surfaces exposed to the cold, sometimes it shivers, while the skin breaks out in goose pimples – and I'm still inside, where it is relatively warm compared to the freezing temperatures outside. One would think that cold is the active element, penetrating all the cracks and openings in the house and pressing against the outside walls, so that they are cooled down even on the inside. But in fact it is the other way round, heat is the active one, it is heat that flows out into the cold, where it immediately dissolves amid the vast masses of cold air and vanishes. It is as if the small amount of hot air doesn't know its own limitations and wants to try heating the air outside, without realising or understanding that it stretches for miles in every direction, including upwards, where it becomes colder the closer it gets to outer space. But it isn't hubris, it's thermodynamics. If two different temperatures come into contact, they will seek to equalise each other. It is like a fall. Outside the temperature sinks, and no more than water can prevent itself from flowing down to the lowest point in the landscape and there becoming part of the great ocean can heat prevent the fall into coldness. This morning I put a bag of empty bottles outside the door, intending to take them down to the recycling station later on, then they were warm, but a few minutes later they were as cold as the ground. This force, the force of equalisation, that two different quantities can't exist side by side, but have to pull and tear at each other until they are equal, doesn't apply only to temperatures, but also to other processes, such as conflagrations, rust, erosion, decay, which occur at varying paces but all work towards the same objective: to make everything the same. The car in the driveway will slowly rust to pieces until it no longer exists, as the mountains will slowly erode until they no longer exist, as all the living bodies in and around the house will one day die and decay until they no longer exist. That too is a fall, from being someone, a body with clearly demarcated boundaries, to being scattered to the winds and being no one. Life can be defined as a battle against the forces for equalisation, which in the long term it is bound to lose. Thus, life exists out of defiance and is tragic by its very nature. In tragedy the fall is apparent from the very first to all except its protagonists, and the tragedy is really nothing but the recounting of how that insight into the inevitable reaches them. Death and nothingness await us, but we fall towards them so slowly that we don't notice it and don't stop to consider that it is them we seek to keep away when we insulate our houses, so that the heat stays within its walls, as in a pool. The cities in the northern countries are made up of these heated pools and towers, the cars are like little ponds of heat, and it is difficult to see these attempts to keep the heat enclosed in small spaces as anything other than beautiful, filled with a particular contrarian dignity, for the space in which they occur is not only black and freezing cold and endless, it is also expanding.

Fireworks

I love fireworks. But not the fireworks that belong on the ground or just above the ground, like firecrackers, Christmas crackers, sparklers, ground spinners or fountains, my love of fireworks only extends to the kinds that are shot up in a rocket, and which unfold in all their glory high, high up in the night sky. Those I have loved for as long as I can remember. I grew up on a housing development, that is to say in the middle of a long row of identical houses with identical driveways, surrounded by gardens of exactly the same size, and although all kinds of things probably went on within their walls, the life that was visible was pretty identical too. The great exception was New Year's Eve, during the hours around midnight, particularly in the final minutes before and the first minutes after, when all the children stood close together with their mother out in the garden and watched their father bending over a launch pad, fiddling until he managed to light the fuse, leaping back and standing with the others to watch the rocket lift from the ground, rise through the air and fling out its crackling flowers of flame so high up that it was visible not only to the little family assembled out of sight of everyone else, close to the back wall of the house, but also to all the other residents of the housing development, allowing them to demonstrate, once a year, what kind of stuff they were made of, who they really were. Oh yes! All those fantastic colours, all that brightly coloured glitter, which not only unfolded explosively, but remained suspended, seeming to descend slowly, there on the black night sky, made it clear to everyone whom they were dealing with. At least that's how it seemed to my father. When the crackle and pop of the first rockets began above the houses early in the evening, he just shook his head and remained in his chair, as opposed to my brother and me, who rushed to the window to look – it had to be the neighbour on the corner up the road, who didn't have the patience, who couldn't wait, didn't know how it should be done. When midnight neared and one rocket after the other rose from the neighbouring plots, he assessed them soberly, sometimes appreciatively, that was a nice one Hansen had there, but also censoriously if there was a whole cascade of fireworks coming from one garden, it was as if they had bought their way to splendour without having deserved it. What a waste of money! he might say then. Other neighbours might fire off only one or two rockets, and not even very spectacular ones at that, and then they were niggardly, humourless. Implicit in all this was the understanding that he, and through him we, our family, knew exactly how it should be done and neither exaggerated nor understated things, neither wasted nor scrimped, but succeeded in doing it perfectly, as all the other families would soon witness, nodding their heads in appreciation. He had set up the laundry rack beforehand, it served as a launch pad for the biggest rockets, and around it stood a few bottles, which the smaller ones were to rise from. I never saw him as happy as during those moments, with the lighter in one hand, the other shielding the fuse, how he stood up abruptly and ran a few steps towards us – ordinarily he never ran – and how his eyes shone in his face when the burning fuse reached the powder and the rocket took off. The small ones first, in ascending order up to the biggest one, which was lit maybe twenty seconds before the clock struck twelve, to crown it all with a huge bang and a gigantic figure like a butterfly on the sky above the housing development at precisely the moment when one year ended and a new year began. That no one ever either praised or criticised our fireworks, which were probably drowned out by all the other launches, didn't matter, for these twenty minutes of each year were filled with such intense joy and power that there was never any doubt that the picture painted by the fireworks on the sky above us, of a world beyond the world for a fleeting moment filled with beauty and riches, was not an illusion, but represented something true: our life too could be like that.

Letter to an Unborn Daughter

1 January. The first day of 2014 has been moist and mild, and empty somehow. Ever since I was small that has been my experience of New Year's Day, that it brought a peculiar feeling of emptiness. This was because the final event of the Christmas holiday, New Year's Eve, was over and nothing in particular was going to happen any more, yet at the same time nothing had really changed; there appeared to be nothing new about the new year, as I had presumably unconsciously expected there to be, rather as I had expected everything to be different on the other side the few times we had crossed the border into another country. This made New Year's Day just about the most ordinary and least spectacular day of the year. That's how it's been today too. But now I appreciate it, for the emptiness is here always, in the open landscape beneath the open sky, it's just that we leave our mark on the day, we turn it into our actions, which, insignificant as they are, somehow fill the emptiness beneath the heavens. Not so today, the first of January 2014.

This is your year, the year you will be born, as 1968 is mine. The others born this year will become your generation, you will meet them at school, in the sixth form, at university, and you will have more in common with them than you have with me, for if your personality and your characteristics are genetic and already formed, it is the time in which they will be tested that will be decisive for what you will think and do, perhaps more than we usually imagine – at least that's what I think.

If I'm not mistaken, there was a science fiction magazine when I was growing up called *1999*. Kubrick's space-age fable was called *2001: A Space Odyssey*. An essay assignment we were sometimes given at school was 'A Day in the Year 2000'. Today is the first day of 2014, which means that I am already far into the future imagined in my childhood. But the only one who looks a little futuristic is you, lying there like an astronaut in black space, with your big helmet, your spindly body and thin limbs, and the line of communication to the mother ship coiled about you, it too floating. On the last ultrasound image we saw of you, you stuck your thumb up at us, and we laughed, you're doing OK in there. There are two months left before your birth. The only worrying thing is that there seems to be something wrong with your foot. The midwife froze the image of it and studied it for a long time, before she moved the ultrasound probe a little, got a new angle and froze that too. It looks like she has a club foot, she said. A club foot? I said. Yes, she said. It isn't dangerous, and something can be done about it. She said you would probably have an operation and would have a brace on your leg. It would be fine and wouldn't mark your life in any way – the only thing, as she put it, was that you might not become a slalom racer when you grow up. They're good at this kind of thing, it won't be a problem, everything will turn out fine. In the evening I called Yngve, my brother, your uncle, and told him. Well, you had that too, he said. A club foot? I said. Did I have a club foot? I'd never heard that before. Yes, he said. That's what you had.

I have lived forty-five years without anyone ever telling me I was born with a club foot. What they did tell me was that there was something wrong with one of my feet when I was born, that it had been put in a cast and later massaged every day, and then it had turned out fine. I'd taken that to mean that it had been a little crooked or something. I called my mother to tell her what they'd said about your foot during the ultrasound scan. It turned out the term 'club foot' had seemed so awful to her that she'd never used it. And it does lead one's thoughts to something medieval, a hobbling bell-ringer in a Gothic church or to Lord Byron, whose club foot is the first thing one thinks of despite his being such an impressive person in so many ways.

But that I myself had had a club foot but my foot turned out so normal that I hadn't even known about it was primarily uplifting news for you and your foot.

You are no longer a foetus, but a tiny infant, fully developed. Sometimes you're awake while your mother is asleep, and sometimes you are asleep while she is awake, as if you were already living your own life in there, in your own little bedsit.

I have picked up a pram and a cot from a friend's place – the pram is in the summer house, the cot in what will be your room – and I've bought a mobile with little planes flying around a sun, it's going to hang above the changing table in the bathroom. Sometimes I think that the only thing missing is you, almost as if we were going to pick you up at the hospital, while in fact you are here with us all the time, in the bathroom, in the bedroom, in the kitchen, in the living room, in the car, in town. The canal separating you from us is only a few centimetres long, but even so it is as if you were in another world. When I look at the pram and the cot I am filled with expectation but also with unease, for they exist for an absent child. That's when I remind myself that you are actually already here. And of the thumb you turned up in there.

JANUARY

Snow

While rain forms part of a continuous movement, in which raindrops gather in puddles, pools, brooks, waterfalls, seas, oceans or in subterranean chambers, then from one point or another evaporate and rise through the air again, snow signifies the temporary cessation of this movement. Snow is rain which for a time is out of circulation, which for a few months is stored here, there and everywhere, as if stockpiled. The transformation from rain to snow is a radical one, since the difference between the properties of water in the two modes is so great, and while I know quite well what causes the transformation, that it has to do with temperature alone and that no will is involved in the process, I still find it hard to understand. It is the absoluteness of it that I am unable to grasp, the definite boundary, that something is liquid on one side of the divide and solid on the other, and that the change of state *always* occurs under given circumstances. In other words, what I find difficult to understand is the regularity, the orderliness of nature. If two cars drive towards each other and collide, every single movement that follows, from the smashing of the headlights to the trajectory of the plastic bottle from the shelf above the boot and forward between the two front seats, will be determined by the velocity and angle of the vehicles – no other outcome is possible or imaginable. The splinter from the windscreen must be flung just there, the bonnet must crumple exactly this way. The same applies to rain when the temperature falls and raindrops turn to snow. Snow is made up of six-sided crystals, and each branch of a snowflake is identical, since they have formed in proximity to each other, where conditions have remained the same, while no two snow crystals are alike, since they have formed in different places, under varying conditions. Even this extreme sensitivity to local variation is regulated by laws of nature. And when snowflakes fill the air above you in vast numbers, like a white flicker against the grey sky, and some of them melt against the warm skin of your face while all the others settle soundlessly on trees and branches, heather and grass around you, it cannot happen in any other way either. And yet this abundance of minute precision, this profusion of separate and unique events, has sameness as its result, for when snow covers the landscape, everything vanishes in white. All the different expressions of the forest, like the tree roots snaking across the naked rock, reddish and shimmering in humid weather, all the yellow and brown pine needles that lie trampled into the soil on the path, and so on into infinity, are gathered by the arrival of snow into a single expression, and over the coming months will express only that: whiteness. Like an orchestra, one might imagine, where every single instrument suddenly begins to play the same note. Anyone who has grown up with snow in the winter knows that note, which can sound even when you are standing in a sunlit garden in the middle of summer and, suddenly filled with inexplicable longing, you imagine an empty forest where the wind drives veils of grainy snow between the unmoving dark tree trunks in the dusk.

Nikolai Astrup

We are visiting my mother in Ålhus in Jølster, a municipality in north-west Norway. Her house lies a stone's throw
from the parsonage where the painter Nikolai Astrup grew
up, and today I went there with the children to go sledging.
They got a snow racer last Christmas, which has been standing here ever since, and dragging it behind us we struggled
through the deep snowdrifts up the gentle incline to the
fence around the pastorage, where our sledging run began.
Everything that we could see, Astrup had painted. The main
house of the parsonage, with its shimmering white walls,
the garden outside, the church below, the valley beyond, the
mountains above. And they are not just any old paintings,
but paintings aglow with colour and simplified planes which
give them a powerful radiance, and which no other art or
literature from this part of the country have ever come close
to rivalling. His paintings are entirely devoid of psychology,
which set Astrup off from his contemporary Edvard Munch,
they radiate neither loneliness nor vitality, neither dejection
nor high spirits, but seem somehow cut off from the emotions of the man who painted them, and yet that doesn't lead
them to turn to the landscape itself, to capture its essence
or the feelings emanating from it. Though Astrup lived in

Jølster nearly his whole life and painted almost exclusively local motifs, his paintings are not characterised by familiarity either; none of them could have been titled 'From My Native District', though all of them were just that. That's why I could struggle through the snow with the kids, surrounded by Astrup motifs on all sides, without thinking about it even once. It wasn't because he painted them a hundred years ago; with the exception of the heavily used road that runs past and a few new houses here and there, almost everything here is as it was then. The landscape over which the snow fell so softly and heavily this lead-grey morning was the same as the one he had painted, both the shape of the mountains vanishing into the low cloud cover and the grey surface of the water, which could barely be distinguished now from the fog hanging over it, and yet it was as if there were no points of contact between them. We went in again after less than an hour, the children were exhausted, unused to being outdoors for so long at a time, at least not in that way, and I thought of my own childhood, how we were outdoors from morning till evening and didn't come inside until the darkness was so dense we could hardly see each other. A shadow of sorrow followed the thought, but it had to come from my lost childhood, not theirs, for they seemed pretty happy as they kicked off their boots and hung their wet waterproof trousers on the pegs, faces aglow, before going off to their iPads. After dinner I sat for a while looking at my mother's bookcase, then pulled out a book about Astrup and began leafing through it. That's when it struck me that he had painted this whole world, and that I had grown up among these paintings – we had a reproduction hanging on the wall at home, and my maternal grandparents had another in their living room – without them ever having influenced my experience of it. It was as if he had painted in a parallel universe, a world that existed side by side with this one. In the book I read that he had meticulously written down everything he could see from the parsonage in a notebook. Shrub after shrub, tree after tree, house after house, shed after shed. But only those that had been there in his childhood. Everything that appeared later he had omitted. Was that the parallel universe? Was that what he painted? Childhood is merely an abyss if one is standing far away from it. If one is standing within it, childhood is colour and planes, and to Astrup it must have been as if he were seeing it through a windowpane that he was pressing his face against.

The surprising thing about the ear is that it's so mechanical. With its membranes, fine bones, channels and little fluid-filled cavities it is easy to imagine it being constructed in a workshop for precision mechanics – a bench with the tiny, highly polished and greased anvil lying next to the stirrup and the considerably larger but still miniature cochlea, perhaps on a white rag that the smith, bent over the task of laying a little carpet of fibres inside the posterior semicircular canal, has placed there in order to see the objects better and to prevent the dirt and grime of the bench from sticking to them – which is unimaginable in the case of the other sense organs, the eye for instance, or the mouth. This is of course because sound is a mechanical phenomenon. Something causes the air to oscillate, and this oscillation travels through space like circles on a pond at a speed of about three hundred and fifty metres per second on a middling warm summer's day. These waves, which are invisible to the eye but still physical realities, are led into the head following a funnel principle, in which the outer ear, a round, faintly inclined disk of cartilage of which there is one on either side of the head at roughly the same level as the nose, guide the sound waves into a channel, where they hit a thin wall and die down. But their force, which is contained in the blow as they strike the wall, lives on in a kind of domino-like existence, for the tremor in the wall is propagated and becomes a tremor in some extremely finely modelled bones, and travels onward through fluid-filled channels, which also quiver and tremble, until the movement reaches the little chamber into which all the nerve threads run in a kind of sensory carpet, which turns it into electrical impulses that rush into the brain along little cables at the speed of light.

Surely all children have once seen someone working a long distance away – for example a figure striking a boulder with a sledgehammer – and wondered that the sound is asynchronous with the movement. Soundlessly the sledgehammer strikes the rock, while the crack only arrives the second after. But that isn't all: sound also ricochets and is heard several times in a row, CLACK-CLACK! and then fainter, CLACK-CLACK, CLACK-CLACK. The feeling I got when I realised that sound too was physical, something that travelled through space, was one of clarity, that the world didn't hold any secrets, had no depth, but that everything in it was open and clear as water in a stream, as snow-covered fields, as star-strewn skies at night.

But if the complex which makes up the organ of hearing is mechanical in nature, it is also vulnerable and susceptible to error, both because it is so finely tuned, being connected via all its channels to the rest of the outer skull, the nose, the throat and the mouth, and because it also performs tasks other than the conveying of sound, including balance and orientation, by means of the tiny crystals that lie in one of the channels of the inner ear, the so-called otoliths or ear stones, which move around on another sensory carpet every time the head is tilted, so that the position of the head is continually registered.

What simple creatures human beings are! Some highly mobile membranes and fine bones cause us to hear. A few little stones in our ear help us stay upright in the world. In that sense we are not so distant from the dinosaurs that to help them digest swallowed huge stones which remained in their bellies knocking against each other as they walked, grinding the food between their surfaces. When the stones had been ground down, they vomited them up and swallowed new ones. It may have been primitive, but it also shows how narrow the gap between the material world and living creatures can be. For that's how it is: life has always used every available means to persist here, and has always incorporated elements of the material world into its continual processes of refinement. Electricity through nerves, water in hollows, stones in the ear.

Björn

Björn's face is long and nearly rectangular, the chin protrudes slightly, the cheekbones are high but not very pronounced, the mouth seems a little crooked, perhaps because he often purses his lips, as if he were sucking on something. His eyes are blue, his gaze is mild and amiable. The most characteristic thing about Björn is maybe his way of walking, he does it so lightly, as if he weighed almost nothing and weren't fastened to the ground but floated above it. A gust of wind might seize hold of him at any time, that's the impression I get when I see him walking across the lawn towards the house where I am sitting, or on the country roads out here, or in the streets in town. I never mistake his figure, even if I see him from behind at a distance of a hundred metres in the middle of a crowd: there's Björn. The lightness of his gait is not primarily elegant, he is tall and has long limbs, which seem to swing about loosely, but rather ethereal, closer to air than to earth, as if, had he been able to, he might at any time fling out his arms and, flapping them slowly like a crane or a pelican, rise through the air. He always dresses elegantly however, in shirts, lambswool sweaters, neckerchiefs, suits, topcoats, yet casually, in the sense that the almost upper-class air of this style of dress doesn't weigh him down, doesn't represent any kind of burden on him but is something he wears with great naturalness. If one is in the same room with him, one quickly discovers that his elegance is not unqualified, but deceptive and threadbare – his suit jackets are crumpled, often dirty, as if he had been working out in the garden in them, his shirts are flecked with food scraps, from egg or sauces, for example, and his hair, once blond, now darker, is always dishevelled. He likes to talk, and it doesn't matter about what, it seems, the important thing is that he is sitting with someone and isn't alone. If he is allowed to direct the conversation, it will often turn to history, especially military history, Swedish and German and Russian, from the seventeenth century up to our own time, natural science, especially astronomy, and geopolitics. His words carry weight, for he knows a lot and he has travelled around the world and seen the most outlandish places, but he rarely throws his weight around, he never dominates a conversation; dominance and authority are alien to his character. If conflicts arise around him, he tries to minimise or ignore them, and if that doesn't work, he walks away. That he craves company (Why? What is it that he can't bear being alone with?) and at the same time can't stand conflicts or dominance is what must make him so restless, so unbound, so light. His nature is mild, his soul is amiable, but his evasiveness and reluctance to commit himself must still have harmed others, irresponsibility always does sooner or later. Björn is sixty years old, but there is nothing settled or rigid about him, his restlessness is too great for that. The only old-mannish thing about him is his sweet tooth. He puts three spoons of sugar in his coffee and always has a bite of something sweet near at hand.

When I am sitting with him and for some reason or other look down or away and then abruptly glance back at him, there is always a smile playing on his lips, as if he knows something about me that I myself haven't the slightest idea about.

The Otter

The otter has round black eyes, a conspicuous semicircular nose and a long mouth, the corners of which point down. The shape of the mouth makes the otter look disgruntled or angry, sometimes also sad. The same goes for its gaze, which is often what crime novels call 'gimlet-eyed' but which at times can also seem mournful. The whiskers below the nose resemble a skimpy moustache, while the eyes are protuberant and emphasise the low brow. All this still doesn't say much about the otter's appearance, since this is linked to such a large extent to movement, speed, litheness, shyness, all of which are qualities that recast its facial features or hide them so well that they practically disappear. One winter I had an otter as my companion, I saw it regularly over nearly three months, often at dusk or at dawn, but it was never close enough or immobile enough for me to get a clear picture of its face. It seemed to merge with the way it moved, which again merged with its being, the impression that remained with me when it had gone. Something restless, for it was always on its way somewhere, something systematically searching, for it seemed to keep the whole landscape under surveillance while it moved, stopping occasionally to have a look around, which contrasted with its low centre of gravity – the otter has short legs and is strikingly long in relation to its height, and this at times scurrying, almost wriggling pattern of movement seems so oriented towards the ground, as if the ground, which it barely appears to have left and almost seems to be a part of, were its real domain – something tall and stately came over it then, when it craned its neck and looked out towards the western horizon or east towards the inner islands. At other times, crossing longer, more open stretches, there was something lumbering and jerky about its movements, not unlike the running gait of a marten, which is in fact a relative of the otter. In the water, with only its head sticking up, it looked like a little seal.

I arrived at the island on a January afternoon, it was already dark as I stepped ashore onto the jetty, and unusually cold for this part of the coast, fifteen degrees below zero. I had rented a house there, the furnishings of which seemed to have been preserved intact since the 1950s, and that first night, before I had got the place warmed up, I lay with my clothes on beneath three duvets on the sofa in the living room. There were only four other people living on the island, a family of three, who for the most part stayed indoors, and a recluse who lived in the loft of one of the boathouses; I didn't become aware of his presence until several weeks later. It was a small island, and I soon got to know it in detail during my walks criss-crossing it in every direction. I saw the otter for the first time beneath the light of the solitary lamp over the jetty below the house, it must have come up from the sea, now it stood there shaking off water. I followed it with my eyes as it moved in a series of little hops out of the glare of the light and into the darkness on the island. The next time I saw it was on the other side of the island, then it was swimming maybe twenty metres from the shore. The sea was perfectly still, and the snow lying in every hollow and on every expanse along the smooth rock slopes made the water seem completely black. The otter slunk up a bluff a little way off, stopped and stared at me, gave one leap and vanished. There was something solitary about it, I always saw it alone, and always heading somewhere, as if it had a large territory to cover, like a sentinel or an inspector, in a world where it was the only one of its kind. Most often I saw the otter down by the jetty, from the window, and the sight made me happy, I bonded with it in a way, we were out here together. Except for a phone conversation with my mother once a week, I didn't speak to anyone. A couple of times the island was covered in snow, then I walked around looking for its tracks. The ones I found often ran along the same routes and always ended at the water's edge. Then, on a bright and sunny morning, I discovered something which looked like a kind of slide in the snow, a track which ran down along the inside of one of the smooth rock slopes. It made me curious, and over the following days I stopped at the slope on my walks to see if it might be what I thought. And it was. One afternoon the otter appeared on a bluff, I was standing far away but with the dark blue sky as a backdrop I saw its silhouette clearly. It ran down to the track, and from there it slid down to the bottom, before it slipped out into the water, ducked under and disappeared from view. There was no practical reason for it to go down the slide, so it must have done it for fun, for the sheer joy of it. And that thought, that this solitary rapacious predator could suddenly rise above its narrowly circumscribed instinctive existence and enjoy life, shone like a light within me and was the first hint of the slow ascent from the darkness that the next few weeks would bring.

The Social Realm

The winter months that I spent on the little island far out at sea were almost entirely without event. I arrived there from a city where things were happening all the time, both on the margins of the life I was living – all the people in their cars, on buses, walking across squares, in and out of houses and shops – and in the middle of it: breakfasts, dinners and TV evenings with the woman I was married to, constant phone conversations, constant meetings, constant parties. On the deserted island there was none of this. The first weeks the absence felt like a craving for something, something I needed with my entire being but couldn't have. Hence there was nothing restful about being there, for all the silence and eventlessness did was to open up new space for my disquiet, which seemed to hurtle about within me. One doesn't notice how great the power of the social realm is until it is taken away, rather as a drug addict doesn't know the power of heroin until there is none. At the same time, it is within the lonely individual and the drug addict that the battle is fought, heroin and the social realm exist independently of them and are as passive as they are indifferent to them.

So I needed other people, their absence tugged and tore at me. But what did I need them for? To see me? To touch me? To acknowledge me? I disliked being touched, so it wasn't that, but I wanted to be seen and I always sought acknowledgement – and yet that wasn't it either, for as a writer one can be both seen and acknowledged without meeting a single person. So what was it?

The powerful need for others, which seemed to stand up and shout within me when I walked around inside the empty house or walked around on the empty island, gradually weakened, and could be gone entirely for hours at a time, eventually even for days. Since our inner world is never empty or silent, not even when we are asleep, but always filled with impressions, thoughts and emotions, something else seeped into the space that had previously been occupied first by the social realm, then by the urge for the social realm. These were the non-social events. They were just as rich and complex but of an entirely different nature. It was the wall of clouds that gathered on the horizon and made the ocean beneath turn black when it came drifting in towards land. It was the clatter of the chains and the snapping of the ropes and flag lines in the harbour when a wind blew up. It was the whine of the wind around the corners of the houses, it was the faint booming of the waves from the other side of the island. It was the fish hook lying for a moment on my palm, its three rusty but sharp points against the skin of my hand, reddish from the cold salt water. It was the smell of the soap that reminded me so strongly of a soap from my childhood, it was the two fish in the shiny sink in the kitchen which suddenly began to thrash about. It was the old hard snow crust in the hollows that got covered in new snow and made me think of the relationship between grandparents and grandchildren. None of this was enough, the urge for more was constantly rising in me, but it was still a lot, so what was missing?

There was no answer. The fish hook, with its smooth little appendage of seaweed, was beautiful as it lay on my reddish palm, but it didn't answer to anything within me, nor did it respond to anything I did, other than in a purely mechanical sense, such as floating in a long arc of thirty metres through the air and piercing the hard surface of the water with a little splash when I made a cast with the rod, or clattering against the rock when I had reeled it almost all the way in and gave the rod a final jerk, when the water seemed to suddenly let go of it, and it flew up and landed behind me. Being out there became an exercise in not expecting an answer, not expecting any response, but just accepting that everything existed in its own right, that any interaction was purely mechanical. What I learned was that the expectation of an answer runs so deep that it is presumably fundamentally human, the most characteristic trait of our nature. And what I now see is that the new virtual world that our children are growing up in is so addictive precisely because it satisfies the need for reply and response, and because it does so immediately. In this way the virtual penetrates to the core of the social and provides us with all the rewards of the social realm without requiring us to pay the corresponding price, so that we can now sit entirely alone, on our own island, without the mechanical interaction ever causing the urge for other human beings to rise within us and tear wildly about like a recently caught animal in a cage.

The Funeral Procession

One morning when I came down to the living room in the house out on the island, a boat had moored at the furthest jetty. It was snowing and a strong gale was blowing, the snowflakes chased along nearly horizontally in the air, and visibility was poor, yet I had no difficulty seeing that it was an ambulance boat. Until then I hadn't known that ambulance boats existed, but of course they must, considering how many islands there are along the coast, and how often their inhabitants must need an ambulance service for matters that aren't serious or acute enough to warrant one of the costly helicopter ambulances.

The water in the bay was jet black, and the landscape rising up in a V on both sides of it was grey and white. The boat bobbed on the waves, tugging at its moorings like a dog on a leash. I went into the kitchen and made myself some sandwiches. When I came back into the living room with a plate in one hand and a glass of water in the other, I saw a procession of four people walking down the narrow road. Two of them carried a stretcher between them. The patient was covered with some kind of blanket, it was black and looked rather like a sheath. I thought it might be a special piece of equipment for medical transportation by boat, that the sea was so rough at times that ordinary blankets or duvets for the patients were inadequate, that they had to be waterproof. They disappeared behind the walls of the boathouse for a moment, then reappeared on the jetty itself and walked over to the boat. Though the figures were clearly outlined against the moving background of whirling snowflakes and drifting clouds, there was something blurry about them, as if they and not the snowflakes were flickering. Yes, there was something ghostly about these four figures carrying a fifth, just as there was something ghostly about the boathouses, looming with their gaping windows and doors, and about the jetty with its cranes, as if they were just about to shift into another dimension. Yet it was only when they stopped in front of the boat and lowered the stretcher, and one of the men made a gesture over the figure lying on it, or rather over the bag – it looked like he was closing the upper part with a zipper – that I understood what was happening, that the body they were carrying was dead, and that they were there to ferry it to the mainland.

They bowed. Then they lifted the stretcher and carried it on board. The engine was started, the moorings untied, and shortly afterwards the boat backed out, turned slowly and headed out across the sound at low speed beneath the heavy grey sky, from which an infinity of new snowflakes came drifting in this extravagant abundance of lifelessness and cold.

While the fourth man, who had remained on the jetty, began walking back along the road and was soon hidden by the boathouses, I followed the boat with my eyes, half expecting it to continue at trolling speed, out of respect for the dead, but as soon as it had cleared the shoals, it sped up, giving rise to that curious effect which occurs when the drone of an engine increases and grows stronger, and at the same time, since it is moving away, also becomes fainter. As the boat was swallowed up by all the grey, I thought that that is exactly how death is.

Crows

Crows are grey birds with black heads, black wings, black beaks and black claws. Like owls, they have been associated with death from early times, but for different reasons, for while the owl with its soundless flight and its secretive being belongs to the night and mystery, the crow is ubiquitous and by nature loud, almost swaggering. The black head resembles a hood pulled down over the grey breast and the grey back, not unlike the hoods once used by executioners, and together with the sounds they produce, closer to screams than to song, the hoarse and raucous *kra kra kra*, there is something unpleasant about them, which one can't say about owls, so if both forebode death, it must be different deaths, or different aspects of death. Perhaps the owls have to do with the actual transition from one state to another, as they glide through the forest at twilight or dawn, as if between the night of the hereafter and the day of the living, while the crows, so visible and so audible, express the hideous, physical, corporeally present side of death. That the crow doesn't seem to make a secret of anything, and in that way also embodies it, I mean not just hideousness glimpsed here and there, but a hideousness that displays itself with no shame, also reminds one of the dead body, which is no longer able to conceal anything but is condemned to show all.

I saw a crow this very morning, it was standing at the roundabout just outside Ystad staring at the cars as I drove the children to school. Normally there aren't many crows in this landscape – or rather there are, but they are of a different kind than the grey and black ones that I grew up with; the crows here are smaller and entirely black, for a long time I thought they were jackdaws, but their beaks are light-coloured, while these ones have black beaks, so they must be rooks, I've concluded. They behave quite differently from the hooded crows, they appear in enormous flocks of several hundred, and every evening they come flying in over the rooftops, in the spaces between the tree crowns – which in summer, when the trees are densely covered in leaves and shimmer greenly in the sunlight, is a pretty sight, but which now, when the branches are bare and the colours of the landscape are grey and brownish, has something barren and hopeless about it – on their way to the place where they spend the night, some huge trees lining an avenue maybe a hundred metres from our house. Every evening they saturate the air with their screeching and chattering, building a kind of sonic dome around themselves, and while at first I found it unsettling, for the sounds seem to issue from a single creature, unable to find peace out there in the darkness, now it has turned into something comforting, a confirmation that everything is as it should be.

So why has the crow in particular come to represent the unpleasant and the ominous when there are so many other hideous creatures to choose from?

The same holds for the crow as for the owl: something

about it reminds one of human beings, drawing it closer to our world than a worm, a frog or a gull. The crow I saw this morning started to walk across the whitish-yellow grass as we drove past it, and because its wings were black and its body grey, it looked like it was walking with its hands held behind its back, nodding to itself. I smiled, remembering another crow in my life. It lived in the area around my grand-parents' farm. My mother's father, who assigned particular characteristics and meanings to all birds, had a strong dis-like of crows bordering on hatred, and earlier, when he was still going strong, he would sometimes shoot them with his gun. When he tried to shoot this crow, he didn't hit it prop-erly, the shot just tore off its leg. The crow lived on for several years with one leg and was often seen around the farm. Maybe it had forgotten what my grandfather once did to it, but I have always imagined that the memory was burned into it, and that it stood like Captain Ahab up in the tree, fol-lowing my grandfather with its eyes as he wandered slowly past beneath it, on his way to the cowshed in the dusk.

Setting Limits

I am beside myself. The agitation is like a deficiency, a sudden want, as if something had been torn away from me and my body wants it back. My emotions toss this way and that, hitting the walls within me. They only do this when the balance between myself and other people has been upset. When someone wants something and I say no. Or when someone says no and I still force them to do what I want. Both are things I shy away from, saying no and forcing my will on someone who is unwilling. This is what weakness is, to be so sensitive to the will of others that one doesn't dare defy them. The archetypical encounter between one's own will and that of others is the one between parents and children; this is the bond where our relation to will gets established, what follows are modifications. That's why I'm distraught. About an hour ago we were going to have lunch, one of the children didn't want to sit down with us, instead she went out into the hall and put on her boots and a rain jacket, she was going down to the shop to buy Saturday sweets. I told her she could do it afterwards, but not now, we were going to eat. She said she wasn't hungry. I said fine, but that she still had to sit with us. She said no, and opened the door. I grabbed her around the waist, pulled her in, she tried to hold on to the door frame, I dragged her through the hall and into the dining room, she kicked and thrashed, tried once again to hold on to something, but I tore her loose and set her down in her seat by the table, where the others sat silently, looking at us. You're going to sit here until we're done eating, I said. She made a face, imitating the movements of my mouth, she didn't want to lose face in front of her siblings, but I could see that there were tears in her eyes. She turned in her chair, so that she faced the other way. We ate, no one said anything. Suddenly she turned back, put food on her plate, started to eat with exaggerated wildness, rice scattered across the table, her knife and fork clattered against the plate. I told her to stop, she said, I'm eating, isn't that what you wanted? Yes, I said, but you have to eat properly. I'll eat the way I want, she said. Her eyes were still moist. As soon as the last person had finished eating, she stood up, marched out, slammed the door, went past the window, disappeared. I cleared the table and came out here. One of the most important tasks of parents is to set limits for their children, not because what children do when they go too far is necessarily dangerous in itself, but so they know that limits exist, that everything isn't wide open, for the open and limitless is unsafe, out there they are on their own, so that setting limits, establishing routines and laying down rules is to make them feel safe, to make the world seem recognisable and manageable. At the same time one of the worst things parents can do to their children is to humiliate them, make them lose face, feel powerless. That's what I just did. And it hurts to know it. She is hurt too, but for the opposite reason. I know how that feels, few memories are more powerful within me than those in which my father humiliated me by forcing his will on me, bringing me to my knees for some trifle or other, how weak and worthless I felt at such times, when I wept and fought against him with no hope of winning, since his will was so much stronger than anything I had in me.

All I want now is to make things right again. But if I go in to see her and try to explain, she'll just stick her fingers in her ears, she wants to have even her humiliation to herself. So what I am going to do is to get out a hammer and some of those little staples that one uses to fasten cables to the wall, and put up the lamp that for several months now I've been promising to hang from the ceiling of her room. It is made up of a long row of little round paper lanterns in various colours and will hang above her bed like a garland.

The Crypt

The same year that the third great Viking ship found in Norway was excavated, at Oseberg, the town of Ålesund burned. At that time the Viking ships were displayed in makeshift exhibition halls, and the great Ålesund fire hastened the process of building a separate museum for them. The architect Fritz Holland proposed building an enormous crypt for them beneath the royal palace in Oslo. It was to be 63 metres long and 15 metres wide, with a niche for each ship. The walls were to be covered with reliefs of Viking motifs. Drawings exist of this underground hall. It is full of arches and vaults, and everything is made of stone. The ships stand in a kind of depression in the floor. More than anything it resembles a burial chamber, and that is fitting, one might think, both because the three ships were originally graves and because placed in a subterranean crypt beneath the palace gardens they would appear as what they represented: an embodiment of a national myth, in reality relics of a bygone era, alive only in the symbolic realm. The crypt was never built, and the power of history over the construction of national identity has since faded away almost entirely. There is another unrealised drawing of Oslo, from the 1920s, with tall brick buildings like skyscrapers along the main thoroughfare, Karl Johans Gate, and Zeppelins sailing above the city. When I look at these drawings, of a reality that was never realised, and feel the enormous pull they exert, which I am unable to explain, I know that the people living in Kristiania in 1904, as Oslo was called then, would have stared open-mouthed at nearly everything that surrounds us today and which we hardly notice, unable to believe their eyes. What is a stone crypt compared to a telephone that shows living pictures? What is the writing down of *Draumkvedet* (*The Dream Poem*), a late-medieval Norwegian visionary ballad, compared to a robot lawnmower that cuts the grass automatically?

Since the art of narration is fundamentally about credibility, few stories are more difficult to pull off than counterfactual ones. While stories set in parallel realities or in the future are in principle entirely detached from events in our world, and in that sense are free, counterfactual stories are closely connected with them, and what they demand of us, that we disregard everything we know and let this massive and extensive knowledge weigh less than a single line of reasoning in a single book, is difficult to comply with. On the other hand, every single moment of life stands open in several directions, it is as if it had three or seven doors, as in a fairy tale, into rooms that all contain different futures. These hypothetical offshoots of time cease to exist whenever we make a choice, and have never existed in themselves, a little like the unknown faces we see in dreams. While the past is lost for ever, everything that didn't happen in it is doubly lost. This creates a particular kind of feeling of loss, the melancholy of an unrealised past. The feeling sounds overwrought and unnecessary, something to fill our idle and sheltered souls, but it is founded on a fundamentally human insight and longing: everything could have been different.

Autumn is a transition, a time of emptying – of the light in the sky, the warmth in the air, the leaves on the trees and plants. The winter that follows is a state in which immobility reigns. The earth stiffens, water freezes to ice, snow covers the ground. That this state is sometimes personified as a king is perhaps due to a feeling that the immobility is something imposed, something that comes from the outside and forces itself upon the landscape. King Winter, he is called, and when I think of him, I can't help pondering what his relation is to another kingly personification, namely King Alcohol. Two majesties of destruction, two emptiers of the world, two inflicters of immobility. One on a grand scale, whole countries and realms, the other on a smaller scale, a person here and there. But do they really have anything in common? Doesn't King Alcohol reign over intoxication and the unbounded life, isn't he the monarch of exultation? When drunkenness arrives in the blood, isn't it as if the eyes light up and an inner warmth softens the features, yes, as if life comes flowing with it? Whereas with winter what arrives is the cold, which unlike alcohol stops or slows down all processes? It appears that way. But King Alcohol is an illusionist; the life that suddenly shines in the eyes is merely a semblance, it resembles life, but it isn't, and in this way it is connected with winter, which is also a stage for lifelike events. When sunlight is flung out over a white landscape on a clear, freezing winter day, and the snow glitters and beckons in millions of facets, or the greenish Northern Lights travel in waves across the night sky, they stand in such glaring contrast to the immobility that reigns everywhere else in the landscape that they are easily misinterpreted as an expression of life and the living. But the light is cold, it awakens nothing, penetrates nothing, what we see is merely a mechanical reflection. Few describe the life-lessness of winter more eerily than Dante in *La Divina Commedia*, in which the inner circle of hell is depicted as an enormous lake covered in ice, where the dead are frozen fast with only their heads above the surface. They can't move, even the tears in their eyes are immobile, frozen. The only things they are still able to move are their mouths. They can use them to hurl curses or express their remorse, but since they can't back up their words with their bodies, the words carry no weight, they mean nothing. It makes me think of drunks shouting at passers-by in the street or confiding in a stranger on a park bench, for while their words may express anger, despair, joy or sincerity, they never have any consequences, they are stuck there, in their life on the streets. The intoxica-tion that gives them joy also keeps them prisoner. That is how I remember my father in his final years, trapped in something he couldn't get out of. His winter was endless, it snowed and cold winds blew everywhere, not just outside the house he sat in, but inside it too. That's how I imagine it. That it snowed and blew in his bedroom, on the stairs, in the kitchen, in the living room. That there was winter in his soul, winter in his mind, winter in his heart.

Sexual Desire

Sexual desire belongs among the basic sensations, along with hunger, thirst and fatigue, and its structure is identical to theirs. Something is missing, and that lack is manifested in the body in the form of a powerful, more or less intense craving, which one knows can only be satisfied by giving the body what it demands: food, drink, sleep, sex. But while hunger, thirst and fatigue are states characterised by increasing pain which lead to death unless the needs they signal are fulfilled, and may therefore be called sensations of scarcity, sexual desire is a pleasurable state, it is essentially characterised by a surplus, and if it remains unstilled, this has no bodily consequences, only emotional ones, such as disappointment, anger, frustration, feelings of inferiority. This is because, unlike the other three primary needs, sexual desire is not about maintaining the basic functions of one's own body, preventing it from dying, but the opposite, creating new life beyond the boundaries of the self. This is why sexual desire can't be satisfied in solitude, but only by involving someone else, and for this reason it is an enormously complicating force in a life and in a culture. Our other basic needs are taken care of through a system of transactions and seem woven into the very fabric of society, with money acting as a kind of intermediary – few of us produce our own food or drink, but we still manage to still our hunger and slake our thirst every day, since we perform one of the many jobs society offers and receive payment in the form of money which we then use to buy food and drink. The same is true of clothes, which prevent us from feeling cold, and housing, which both shelters us from wind and cold and protects our belongings. The most reasonable and democratic course of action would therefore be to incorporate the urge to procreate into this system, so that one could purchase sex when aroused, just as one buys food when hungry. One could imagine sex stations along major roads, sex markets next to shopping centres outside cities, more exclusive sex boutiques in the city centres. This would place everyone on an equal footing from the start, and one could instead focus one's energies on regulating the economy to reduce the gap between the rich and the poor, where the great structural inequality lies. But faced with such a proposal most of us would baulk, regardless of how closely aligned it is with the social-capitalist way of thinking. We can sell our labour or buy the labour of others, we can live and work in a society where all value is converted into monetary value, where we even pay other people to look after our children, where everything we own and have and do is bought and paid for – just not sex. Why? To understand the role that sexual desire plays in culture, as a thought experiment we can try to remove it. A society in which no one feels sexual desire, and where reproduction is maintained through artificial insemination, what would that look like? The two sexes would become more and more similar, finally merging into one. This single-sexed organism, devoid of desire for any of its fellow creatures, would still have all the other human emotions intact and would feel, for example, warmth and affection for others. But warmth and affection are feelings where nothing is at stake and which are directed towards what is already there. Love seeks only to maintain itself, and the only alternatives are a deepening or a fading away. It would be a society without war, a society without violence, and thus a society in which utopian goodness and security were realised. It would never cross anyone's mind to abduct Helen. It would be a society in which what is now found only in the facade of the middle class would permeate every part, a society where no one had anything to hide, a society without secrets. And sex would be understood rather as we understand cannibalism today, as something barbaric and brutal, an activity that consumes human beings and spreads havoc around itself, containing elements of violence, conquest, ruthlessness and dominance. It would be considered the expression of a system of values where the outer triumphed entirely over the inner and thus ran counter to everything one knew about the worth of human beings, centred on a pleasure that was unknown in all other areas of human life, so explosive that if unchecked it could become the end goal of everything – in short: sex would be a subversive activity, which one sought to control by surrounding it with rules and taboos, shame, euphemisms and lies, until one succeeded, through education and new methods of reproduction, in completely removing it from human life. These new people pat each other encouragingly on the cheek, they are content with their lot, but that is all they have.

Thomas

Thomas's eyes are set deep in their sockets, they are almond-shaped and placed far apart, giving his face a faintly Mongol look. He is partly bald, with hair in a wreath around his temples and at the neck, and he wears a short beard on his chin and below his mouth, while his cheeks are bare. All this makes him look a lot like Lenin, which one thinks about the first few times one meets him but later forgets. Once Thomas told me he was out walking in Stockholm early one Sunday morning, the streets were deserted, he was the only person out. A limousine had come along the road and stopped at the crossroads just in front of him. A man peered out of the rear window, Thomas recognised him, it was Gorbachev. Their eyes met, and Gorbachev lifted his hand in greeting before the limousine continued up the empty street. Thomas laughed as he told the story. Perhaps Gorbachev had noticed something familiar about him and for a brief moment imagined that an old friend was standing there on the pavement, or else he was just honouring the human encounter. Thomas is a photographer, but unlike most photographers he doesn't appear to be interested in the moment, he rarely photographs things that only happen once, and when he does, the moment always expresses something else, something lasting. Yes, Thomas is interested in permanence. And in a strange way this timelessness is also integrated into his personality, for even though he grew up in the 1950s, was young in the 60s and lived his first adult years in the 70s, in Stockholm, along with other photographers who have since become well known, he hardly ever talks about the past; what interests him is always what is happening now. Thomas is easy-going, his personality makes few demands on others, so it is easy to underestimate him, at least in the company of other artists, since he doesn't speak in order to assert himself but only when he has something to say. There is a great darkness in his photographs, they are full of shadows and walls, and there is also a darkness in him, especially in the winter, but not one that is burdensome to others, for even his darkness is undemanding, it doesn't add anything to a social setting but only takes something away, a part of his presence, which at times ceases altogether, as if he were somewhere else. Even though this gives him an air of isolation, he never radiates loneliness. I think he is lonely when he is by himself and filled with darkness, but also that other people draw him out of himself, and that he is so genuinely interested in these encounters that while they last, he lives in them. Thomas's great sorrow is that he doesn't have children, and when I first got to know him I took care not to speak about my own, I was afraid it might be painful to him, but then I realised from the way he talked about my children – the little details he noticed which were representative of their character, what was lasting in them – that he didn't make that kind of connection. Thomas is not an intellectual, few photographers are, he meets the world with his own self without applying any particular theory to it, but that doesn't mean that the world he creates is open, only that it is closed in a personal way. The world he operates in, for instance when he sits here laughing on the sofa in my study and the snuff tucked beneath his upper lip makes it look like he is baring his teeth like a wolf, he keeps open, rather like a road is kept free of snow, and that gives him life, while the loneliness, darkness and death that are inside him close the world that he creates. That is Thomas, he stands in the light and photographs the shadow he casts.

The first sound of the train is a faint rushing, impossible to distinguish from the wind blowing through the trees. Then the warning signal is heard from a nearby crossing, also faint, and one can imagine the barrier booms being lowered, one on either side of the rails, though there isn't a person in sight. We are out walking with the pram, it's winter, the sky is white, the old forest road covered by a thin layer of fine-grained snow which at the faintest breath of wind swirls in varying patterns over the ice in the wheel ruts. The rushing sound rises and is followed by a more compact metallic noise from the movement of the heavy wheels over the rails and an electric hum. Our daughter, who is nearly a year old and is sitting in the pram bundled up in her thick red snowsuit, white hat and white mittens, turns her head. The train moves through the forest, not thundering like the old, square, heavy carriages that serviced this area during the 70s, but rushing, quickly and lightly, surrounded by a swirl of snow. It glides through the faint curve, and the next instant it vanishes behind the trees. Soon the rushing sound is indistinguishable from the wind, and then that too is gone. As we continue along the forest road, I feel uneasy and restless, as if something were wrong. A few minutes pass before I realise that it has to do with the train. The train is going somewhere else, I'm not. It's not hard to dismiss this longing with arguments, for I have sat on that very train, on my way to Malmö, inside the compartments that seen from the outside glow so hypnotically, feeling bored as I looked out at the snow-covered forest, and what did I feel then, if not a longing to live there, in one of the unfamiliar houses glimpsed in passing? I know this as I walk next to the pram along the forest road. But the train's symbolic power is greater than reason, or operates in a different place, and exerts a pull it is difficult to defend oneself against. A plane, which not only is going somewhere else but gets there considerably faster, doesn't have the same aura, nor does the automobile. The escape offered by the car is too common, too everyday, too tied to supermarket shopping trips, while the plane's escape is too realistic, you know that the Istanbul where you will land abruptly after only a few hours' flight will be nearly impossible to connect to. The train's escape, on the other hand, is almost an embodiment of longing, as it winds slowly through the landscape, never stopping long enough in one place for any commitments to be undertaken, and from the windows of which the view is constantly changing, as in a dream. The train never goes from being 'here' to being 'there', and this it has in common with longing, which as soon it reaches 'there' transforms it into 'here', which by its nature it doesn't accept and therefore begins to direct itself towards a new 'there'. And so life goes on.

Georg

Some writers you can't understand until you've met them. That's how it was with Georg. I had tried several times to get an interview with him for various newspapers; every time he referred me to a colleague who he claimed would have plenty to say, unlike himself, who had nothing to say. At that time he was, in the eyes of many, including mine, young and inexperienced as I was, the country's foremost intellectual and its leading poet: no one had written better than he had in the 60s. Not until I asked on behalf of the student radio, which was an idealistic organisation, did he accept. We were planning a festival, and he was going to read from his work. I met him outside the student centre and was to accompany him down to The Cave (Hulen), where the reading would be held. This was on a Saturday, in the morning. It must have been autumn, I remember the blue sky above the hill at Nygårdshøyden and the cold air. I had seen him many times before, a corpulent older man with a beard dressed with conspicuous inelegance, often with a satchel slung diagonally across his chest, walking along the gravel paths towards Sydneshaugen or along the road that runs past the student centre leading to Møhlenpris on the other side of the hill. He appeared to have trouble walking. He was a legend. And in Bergen he had disciples, the people who attended the Retorisk Forum, a group of scholars at the University of Bergen, who called him The Georg or just Georg, to bask in the glory it was to know him, to be on intimate terms with him. They were opposed to romanticism and opposed to Oslo, the capital, opposed to the newspapers, opposed to novels and to any notion of authenticity. They were in favour of classical culture, the expression of cool analytical distance. They were anti-hysterics of a sort, but seen from a distance their admiration for Georg was if not exactly hysterical then at least worshipful. I had never dared attend their meetings, it seemed too much like a sect, I thought you would have to know a very great deal to be part of it. It was a beautiful thing that the country's foremost poet had withdrawn from public life, stopped writing poetry and begun teaching students studying for their first degree in Scandinavian philology. And that one could see him and think, there goes Georg, as if one could actually see everything that had made him a great poet and a brilliant social critic, vastly superior to a writer such as Jens Bjørneboe for example, in terms of argumentation, presumably so superior that it became meaningless to him; better then to teach young people and gather some of them around himself to discuss the ideas he valued. All of this surrounded him on that Saturday when, nearly trembling with awe, I saw him walking up the hill towards the student centre, where we had agreed to meet. He stopped, I introduced myself, we shook hands. And then, at that moment, I understood who he was, or the quality that was most essential to his nature. He had the most sensitive eyes I have seen. They were filled with sorrow, and they took everything in. On the way down the hill towards The Cave I was shaken, I couldn't think of anything else. He himself talked the whole way without ever stopping, amiably and about trivial matters, and I realised that it was his way of coping. He was so close to the world, and he was so close to other people, so full of feelings, that in order to cope he had to establish a permanent, continual distance between himself and everything and everyone. As we walked down the hill, he did this by chatting – leaving no room for me to say anything, even if I had wanted to – as if he had to turn back the inward flow, that everything entered him, with an outward movement of equal force. And his entire aesthetics, with its emphasis on the classical, the rational, the matter-of-fact, dry and non-identical, the non-sentimental, non-emotional and soberly balanced, was also a way for him to survive. He was drawn towards everything in the external world that ran counter to his inner being, and out of this dynamic, this balance, which isn't unusual – I have seen the eyes of another Norwegian writer, Ole Robert Sunde, which are also extremely sensitive, and I know what his writing is like, like the world seen through the wrong end of a telescope – something unusual arises, which is the mark of the very greatest literature: the ecstasy of detachment.

Toothbrushes

The family's toothbrushes are in a cup in the bathroom bristles up, looking a little like flowers in a vase, with their handles like stems and their brushes a kind of corolla. But the impression they give is rather different, of course. A vase of flowers is an expression of freshness – they are so recently cut from their roots that they still have life's moist gleam about them, and the certainty that they can only be beheld in all their glory when fresh does not apply to toothbrushes, for they are made of plastic and synthetic fibres, which will take hundreds of years to break down. And a vase of flowers carries with it something of the freedom and wildness of the world beyond the walls of the house, while toothbrushes are industrially produced, in addition to the fact that their domain is the interior; they rarely leave the bathroom, which is the most secluded room of the house, and they are used to clean the teeth in the mouth, which then becomes a kind of room within the room. And yet, when I see the cup of toothbrushes on the sink below the mirror, what I think of is a vase of flowers, as if inverted, negated, a counter-image to beauty and freedom, which still partakes vaguely both of the beautiful – the colours, synthetic green, synthetic blue, synthetic yellow; the brushes, synthetic bristles, stiff yet flexible, possessing the infinite durability of inorganic whiteness – and of freedom, given the overwhelming number of toothbrushes in the world and the arbitrary position of the individual toothbrush in this endless stream of fellow brushes, not unlike the relation of the single flower to the abundance it derives from. The children of the house recognise this, for while they are at pains to assert their property rights over everything that is theirs and don't allow anyone to use any of their possessions without prior permission, which is sometimes granted only after lengthy negotiations, often involving powerful emotions expressed through shouts, screams, tears, appeals, yet they are indifferent to ownership when it comes to toothbrushes. If they were to be given their own toothbrush, their sense of ownership would dissolve as soon as the toothbrush joined the bouquet of the others; when they shuffle into the bathroom in the evening, their body language expressing reluctance, since they don't want to go to bed, and brushing their teeth is an unmistakable signal that the evening is over and that night is at hand, they just grab any old toothbrush in the cup, pink, light blue, grey, white, it makes no difference; squeeze some toothpaste onto the bristles and start brushing their teeth with mechanical, distracted movements while simultaneously doing something else, looking at themselves in the mirror, running their hand through their hair, staring at their feet, scratching their belly, turning on the tap. Something in me dislikes this, the feeling their sharing produces in me is one of poor hygiene, messiness, confusion, chaos, unhealthiness. It resembles the feeling I get when I read how in the old days peasant families would eat from the same bowl of porridge, or the same bowl of ale would be passed around so everyone could drink from it. The feeling is irrational, since as a family we live so close together anyway; we use the same toilet bowl, we eat the same food, we sit on the same sofa, sometimes sleep in the same bed, use the same hairbrushes and dry our hands on the same towels, and if one of us gets sick, it soon spreads to the others.

Still, surely it can't be right for them to share the same toothbrushes?

Quite often I observe our life here with the gaze of the child protection service or the social welfare office. Isn't it way too messy? Isn't it far too long since we changed the bedding? When was the last time they took a bath? And how much harm did I cause them the last time I got so enraged that I shouted at the top of my lungs, grabbed one of them by the neck and pushed her into her room?

I frequently imagine a representative of these authorities standing next to me, taking notes. Written in red ink in the notebook is the following: Greasy hair. Dirty nails. One of them very angry for no reason, uncontrolled. Another silent, sullen, uncommunicative. And they share toothbrushes. Foster home placement?

When I was growing up we each had our own toothbrush, there was never any doubt about whom it belonged to, and using a different one was unthinkable. We also had fixed bath days, they were written down in a note on the wall, and as far as I remember, mine were Mondays and Thursdays. The toothbrushes reminded me partly of four teenage girls hanging out by the petrol station, partly of four horses peering over a fence. They were primarily associated with duty, perhaps more than anything else, for what other disagreeable task had to be repeated twice a day your whole life through? Gradually the toothbrush also came to be associated with lying. The first time I lied consciously to my father – I remember it as if it happened yesterday because it was so unheard of – was the winter I was ten years old, I was sitting on a chair in the kitchen while he was making some food, and he asked me if I had brushed my teeth, and I replied, after thinking about it for a few seconds, I don't remember. But I did remember, I hadn't brushed them, so it was a lie. He said I had better do it one more time then, to be on the safe side. I did, but I had discovered something, that it was possible to lie about certain things with no risk of being found out. From then on I could say that I had brushed my teeth even if I hadn't. And from then on I have associated not brushing my teeth with freedom. Which of course is why my teeth are so discoloured and yellow, and why I never show them any more, but always smile with my mouth closed, and sometimes even cover my mouth with my hand when I laugh.

The 'I'

The distinctive thing about life, what distinguishes it radically from non-life, living matter from dead matter, is will. A stone wants nothing, a blade of grass wants something. And what life wants, which separates it from non-life by an abyss, is more life. Without this will, the first form of life would simply have died away, so the will to more life must have been there from the beginning, presumably as the constitutive element of this once-new phenomenon. When the cells gathered together in clusters, as another consequence of the will to more life, they had to be coordinated, a form of communication between the individual parts had to arise, and from these signals or impulses hunger and pain developed, which must have been the first two sensations, and a coordination of the cells in relation to them. The basis for the feeling of being an 'I' must lie here, in the space between the desire and its fulfilment, between pain and its avoidance, for there is *something* that desires and wants, and *something* which feels pain and doesn't want to. But what is it?

Initially the sense of self can't have been more than a vague sensation of extent, of a within and a without, and for most living creatures perhaps it is still like that. But the branch of life that we belong to, together with dogs and cats, apes and pigs, has over the course of millennia opened up more and more sensory channels, more and more possibilities of movement, demanding more and more coordination, as we can see from the brain, where all this lies coiled in evolutionary layers, so that the sense of self has evolved too, in that new components have continually been added to it. But the original elements are still there. By means of simple experiments of an almost illusionistic character, one can cause the brain to extend its domain, to trick it into believing that the body's boundaries lie further out than they actually do, and make it feel accordingly. Phantom pains, where the brain continues to feel body parts which are no longer there, can be explained as the reawakening of old nervous pathways, for they are still there even if the arm or foot is gone. But to feel a new area beyond the body's boundaries as one's own is something else, which shows how central the feeling of extension still is and what a primitive and fragile foundation our identity rests on.

If the sense of extension is the primary element of the 'I', the sense of unity is next in importance. While pain originates in the earliest layers of the brain as it has evolved, it is crucial to the sense of identity that it isn't experienced as such – as coming from a simpler and more primitive place, as something alien, reptilian – but rather is felt to be an equally relevant, contemporary and worthy part of the entity we consider ourselves to be. This sense of unity must have been key in allowing an organism to develop from a single cell into one consisting of multiple cells, and has maintained its grip ever since, through the development of ever greater biological complexity in living creatures. That the feeling of unity has no place, can't be traced back to any single location but seems to belong to the whole body even if it originates in the brain and its activity, is what has given rise to the separation of spirit and matter, body and soul, since the only thing the sense of unity can't encompass is itself.

Seen in this light it seems odd that the largest part of the brain, the cerebrum, is in fact divided into two hemispheres which each contain a complete set of centres for the body's perceptions and motor functions. Under normal conditions they are each in charge of their side of the body, but if one of them is damaged, the other half can take over its functions. The two hemispheres communicate with each other via the corpus callosum, through which bundles of nerve fibres pass. If the corpus callosum were damaged and the nerve fibres severed, this would create an organism with two independent brains, each with a will of its own. They would be ignorant of each other's existence and would both attempt to control the entire body, each from its own side. The sense of extent would probably remain intact, but not the sense of unity; a person with two wills would arise – with two 'I's. Would this person feel a sense of belonging with one of its selves, that one of them represented its soul while the other appeared alien? Or would the person alternate between them, being first one and then the other? That this split is a common motif of horror movies, with Jekyll and Hyde as the archetypal figure, tells us something about how essential it is that we seem one person to ourselves, but perhaps even more so to other people. To have a friend, a lover or a child whose personality changes feels threatening. If that happens, we pathologise it and call it schizophrenia or bipolar disorder. There are conditions in which the 'I' abdicates or loosens its hold over its realm and allows all the disparate elements that it contains, the infinite manifoldness of the soul, to do as they please. This is an escape from the task assigned to the 'I', namely to incorporate all the emotions, impulses, thoughts and actions into one continuous whole, regardless of how contradictory they are initially. This struggle of the 'I', which begins when the infant is weaned from the breast and the symbiosis with the mother is broken, and lasts until the adult dies or lets go in demented old age, is really only about constructing a narrative, a story flexible enough to contain everything in a life but also realistic and simple enough to be practical, and which therefore doesn't shy away from plagiarism, deception, lies and denials of obvious truths: for the self, it is always a matter of life and death.

Atoms

One evening some weeks ago the bureau that stands by the wall in the room next to my office caught my attention. It is brown with elaborate carvings, and probably dates back to the late nineteenth century. But what is it made of? I wondered. Wood, obviously, perhaps stained, with fittings, screws and nails of metal. But what do the wood, the stain and the metal consist of? Atoms, I knew that. Minuscule, in themselves invisible particles in such vast numbers that the sum of them made up this tangible piece of furniture.

I stood up and rapped my knuckle against it, pulled out the drawers, nudged it back and forth.

How was it possible?

If what I had learned about atoms was correct, how could they stick together in precisely this form? What governed the way they stuck together, so that finger atoms both formed a finger and stayed in place, and plastic atoms both formed a plastic bag and stayed in place? And how was it possible that the finger and the plastic bag were of such different materials? One was shiny, smooth and thin, the other was thick with a soft exterior, and an interior that was first soft, then hard? How was this decided?

What happened to the atoms if the plastic bag was placed

in a fire? The plastic would melt, but what did melting do to the atoms? And if the root of my nail got infected, what would be the relation between the atoms in the yellowish-green pus and the atoms in my finger? What happened then, in the far depths of the atomic world, where individual particles apparently floated around in empty space at vast distances from each other, viewed in relative terms?

I suddenly realised that I didn't know anything about the world, not even the part of it I was closest to. I had no idea what the things I could see around me were composed of, or why they looked as they did and had the properties that they had. What was red? I didn't know. What was light? Photons, sure, but what were photons? Was it possible to transform one substance into another, quite different one, as the alchemists had once dreamed of doing?

I had no clue, and that realisation, that I really knew nothing about anything, put me into a panic. I visited Amazon and searched for the words 'atoms', 'particle physics', 'radioactivity', 'nuclear power', ordering every introductory work I could find. When the books arrived a few days later, I immediately began to read. In one of them it said that the full stop at the end of a sentence consisted of a hundred billion carbon atoms. If we wanted to see one of them, we would have to enlarge the full stop until it was a hundred metres long. If we wanted to see one of the electrons inside the atom, we would have to make the full stop ten thousand kilometres across.

The relativisation of distance which this entails, that the electrons in our mailbox are as far from the electrons of the writing desk in front of me as I am distant from the stars in the universe, dissolves all notion of dimension, for who knows how large the universe is? It might well be infinitesimal. It might well be located within another and much larger universe, one that is shaped, for example, like a mailbox. The Milky Way might be the comma in a sentence in a newspaper that hasn't been picked up yet. For the notion of time is relative too; four billion years here might be three minutes there. Both the movement inward, towards the subatomic level of reality, and the movement outward, towards the endlessness of space-time, leave us helpless, and seen in that light the monotheistic god seems a more adequate answer to the riddles of existence than science. Everything that is beyond reason is subsumed under God, whose name may not be spoken since God is also beyond language, but is still present within us, since we are created in God's image. A relationship exists, there is no language for it, and when we submit to God that is what we feel, an unimaginable depth of feeling which connects us with everything that exists, everything that was and everything that will be. But what has once been learned cannot be unlearned. Now we live in atomic reality, and we are alone in the world.

Loki

Loki was very beautiful, Snorri Sturluson wrote, and very cunning and deceitful. Loki was no god, he belonged with the jotuns, the Titans of the North, but as Odin's blood brother he stayed among the gods and was treated as one of them. Loki had no cult, there were no places of sacrifice dedicated to him, but he was still one of the most significant figures in Norse mythology. He was someone who made things happen, often by doing what must not under any circumstances be done, the forbidden and the destructive. Loki was best known for having caused the death of Baldr and thereby unleashing the chain of events leading to the end of the world in Ragnarök. This starts with Baldr dreaming that he is going to die, and with Odin travelling to Hel, the underworld, to find out if the dreams are true. When he learns that they really are expecting Baldr there, the gods receive assurances from all living beings that they won't kill Baldr. All except the mistletoe, which Loki gives to Baldr's blind brother Hod, who shoots it at Baldr as they play, and Baldr dies. Since death has hitherto been unknown among the gods, it is as if their entire world were being torn apart. But the rift has been there all along, in the shape of Loki, who comes from the outside, from Utgard, the realm of the unfinished, the undefined and the chaotic, and who carries it with him into the well-ordered world of the gods, an ambivalence which also applies to his body when he transforms himself into a seal, a salmon, a bird or a mare, in the shape of which he gives birth to a foal, thus crossing the boundary not only between human and animal but also between man and woman, mother and father. The death of the immortal Baldr is the beginning of the end: soon the world will perish and all the gods will die in a great final battle in which the sun turns black, the earth sinks into the ocean, brother fights brother, wolves tear into corpses, and the ship made of the fingernails of the dead is unmoored and comes sailing with Loki at the helm. All this is narrated in the *Poetic Edda*, but sparsely and concisely, as if the poems light up small areas of a greater reality. In most of them Loki, like the other figures, is primarily a vehicle for the action, with certain properties linked to his name. There is however a wonderful exception, when Loki enters the scene fully lit, with a psychological complexity generally absent from the mythological stories. The poem is called 'Loki's wrangling' and takes place after Baldr's death, but before Ragnarök. The gods have gathered for a feast at Ægir's, the jotun who rules over the ocean. At first Loki was there with them, but the others lavished praise on Ægir's servants Fimafeng and Eldir, which Loki couldn't stand listening to, so he simply slew Fimafeng and was chased away. The poem begins as Loki returns. 'Then Loki went into the hall,' it says, 'but when they who were there saw who had entered, they were all silent.' Loki pays their silence no mind. He just asks a little contemptuously why they are silent and unable to bring forth a single word. Either they must allow him to sit down, or they will have to throw him out, he says. He knows they can't throw him out, he knows they have to tolerate him, all his self-confidence derives from that fact. Loki is Odin's blood brother, no one can deny him a seat at the table. The scene is highly recognisable. We are all familiar with the unwelcome guest, the unpleasant and troublesome figure, often drunk, who must nevertheless be tolerated since he is related to the others who are present or is their friend. Loki has done something outrageous, now he sits down as if nothing had happened, and the enmity he senses, the hatred and contempt he sees in every gaze directed at him, don't fill him with shame or remorse but have the opposite effect, they stir him up, they set him going, he goes on the attack. He says the worst thing he can think of about each and every one around the table. He says what must not be said but everyone knows to be true. About Ithun he says that she slept with her brother's slayer. About Bragi he says that he is the most cowardly of the gods. About Odin he says that he performed *seidr*, sorcery, in the guise of a witch, and uses the word for the passive party in a homosexual relationship to make clear what he thinks of him. He uses the same word about Heimdall. About Freyja he says that she has slept with everyone in the room. About Njorth he says that he had a child with his sister. To Skathi, Loki says that he killed her father. And to Frigg, Baldr's mother, he says, 'Thou wilt then, Frigg, that further I tell of the ill that now I know; mine is the blame that Baldr no more thou seest ride home to the hall.' After this barrage of insults, in which nothing is said that isn't true but everything said is outrageous, Thor arrives, and with his coming it is as if realism is suspended and mythology reinstated. Thor chases Loki out of the hall,

Loki flees and turns himself into a salmon to hide from his pursuers in the Franang waterfall, but they find him and bind him with his son's eviscerated bowels beneath a snake that drips venom. Loki's wife, Sigyn, holds a bowl beneath the snake, but every time she has to empty it, the drops strike Loki, who flinches so forcefully that the whole earth trembles. This is what causes earthquakes, the narrator explains. Exactly when all this occurs is difficult to say, for mythical time is different from historical time, unconnected to it, and mythical time is also ambivalent – it is as if past, present and future lie side by side, and what hasn't happened yet nevertheless influences what is happening as much as what has already happened. But since earthquakes still occur, our present time must be after Baldr's death but before Ragnarök. So the unheard-of has already happened, the gods have discovered that they are mortal, but the consequences have yet to unfold. The imbalance in the world is still invisible, like the frailty of the ice the moment before the crack appears.

Sugar

Sugar consists of tiny white crystals that crunch between the teeth, melt on the tongue and, despite their unassuming appearance, fill the mouth with a taste that is as distinctive as it is desirable, which is sweetness in its purest form, yes, sweetness itself. When one adds to this the fact that the nutrients in sugar are quickly taken up by the bloodstream and provide the body with immediate energy, as if new strength were injected into it, it is no wonder that there are bags of sugar in every home. In recent decades, however, our relationship to sugar has changed. From being a relatively neutral stimulant it has come to be shunned. While the one-kilo bag of sugar is still found in kitchen cupboards everywhere, it is the only commodity on the shelves that carries a stigma. Neither the wheat flour, the dry yeast, the oatmeal or the baking powder is tainted by unpleasantness, none of these products are perceived as purveyors of poor health and immorality or a poor quality of life, only sugar is seen in this way. Why? How can something as pure, white and unconditionally good as sugar become something suspect practically overnight?

When I was growing up, in the 1970s, sugar was everywhere, there were virtually no restrictions on its use, at least not in our neighbourhood. The sandwich spreads we ate for breakfast, lunch and supper were often sugar-based: nut, banana, chocolate and caramel spreads, jams, syrup. I put three or four spoons of sugar in my tea, I sprinkled sugar on my porridge, sugar on my pancakes and sugar on my waffles. There was sugar in the fruit squash and sugar in the soft drinks, sugar in the cakes and sugar in the buns, sugar in the chewing gum and sugar in the sweets. Several kids in my class put sugar on their slices of white bread, I remember, and both my father's mother and my mother's father would suck on sugar cubes as they drank their coffee. In its abundance sugar resembled petrol, which was also used lavishly back then, and which like sugar is now under a pall of guilt. The 70s were the decade of petrol and sugar, the heyday of unsophisticated and innocent consumption, which had obvious roots in a culture of poverty, the one our grandparents grew up in and which our parents had left behind. It was a frugal culture, not out of principle but out of necessity, and sugar was a simple and cheap pleasure. When wealth came to Norway, with its differentiation of objects and its exaltation of the costly, which in a monetary culture means the exclusive, the rare and the unique, neither petrol – which flowed abundantly into the bowels of the 70s' greedy machines, where it was transformed into primitive power and speed – nor sugar, with its simple form, mass availability and undemanding appeal, had a place other than on the outside, among the others, the masses who like sugar are not differentiated in a monetary culture but simply relegated to a vague and faceless underclass. That this class organised itself into a party of its own was the only truly new thing that happened in Norwegian political life in the 70s and 80s.

And that this political movement, which called itself the Progress Party, demanded lower petrol prices as one of its major policies, was of course no coincidence, nor was the fact that their highly successful first leader, Carl I. Hagen, came to politics from the sugar industry. It is therefore only logical that the Progress Party, its politics and its voters are perceived in roughly the same way as sugar and petrol by society's intellectual and cultural elite: short-term oriented, destructive, immoral, undesirable. Just as logical is it that petrol and sugar began their merger in earnest at about the same time that the Progress Party expanded. I am thinking of the petrol stations, which now, as the Progress Party is in government for the first time, lie like great shiny palaces of sugar along the roads, filled to bursting with raisin buns, wheat buns, chocolate buns, caramel buns, crates of soft drinks and every other sweet delight imaginable.

Letter to a Newborn Daughter

29 January. I am sitting in a room in the hospital in Helsingborg, in a chair beneath the window, it is night, and Linda is sleeping in the next bed, while you are lying in an incubator beside me, dressed in white pyjamas and a white cap, beneath a little blanket, and you too are sleeping. You were born yesterday, in the evening, and everything went fine, even though you arrived more than a month early. You are healthy and well formed, and you don't have a club foot! Both the nurses and the doctor have examined your feet closely, and there is nothing wrong with them. You were awake for maybe an hour after you were born, you stared up at me with your little black eyes as I dressed you in pyjamas while your mother lay exhausted in bed, looking on. I held you close to me, with one hand supporting your neck and head, the other cradling your body, which curled up and was so tiny that my palm covered it almost completely. It was like holding a small animal. To feel the warmth of your body against mine, and to breathe in your smell, which was so lovely and so much like the smell your siblings once had, filled me with a joy greater than any I have known. Since then you have been asleep, mostly. I am going to sleep now too, with you next to me. Tomorrow I am

going to pick up your sisters and brother, who will see you for the first time.

Linda's waters broke in the middle of the night, and since this was much too early and because I had to stay at home to look after the children, they came for her in an ambulance. She was afraid as she sat waiting for it, it was maybe two in the morning, the empty street outside was lit by the yellow glare of the street lights, glittering on the snow that lay by the roadside. The ambulance seemed to glide past the windows, softly and quietly, and Linda put on her big down jacket, I handed her the bag I had packed hastily, and she walked with slow, careful steps over to the ambulance. After I had driven the children to school, I called Linda's mother, and when she arrived I drove to the hospital. The doctors wanted to perform a Caesarean section the next day, but a plucky midwife who was on duty that evening persuaded Linda to give birth naturally, there was no reason not to in her opinion. Soon Linda was lying with an elastic strap around her belly. The room was clinical and full of technical equipment, the metal beds adjustable, in front of the sink there was one dispenser for disinfectant and another one for soap. Shortly after, when the contractions began to quicken and the birth got under way, all of this vanished. Linda was on her knees, with her upper body hanging over the end of the bed. Every time she had a contraction, she grabbed the mask dispensing laughing gas and inhaled deeply. From time to time she shouted into the mask. Waves seemed to ripple through her, and she fell into their rhythm as if into a trance, and the rhythm seemed to transport her to another place, of pain, body, darkness. Her shouts were hollow and seemingly endless, with no beginning or end. They grew darker, more animal, and contained a pain and a despair so great that whatever I did, whether it was wrapping my arms around her and pressing my cheek to hers or rubbing her back, was no more than a feeble, futile ripple on the surface of the deep that engulfed her. She was in the middle of something, in a place I could never reach but only observe from the outside, and yet it changed everything for me too, it was like a tunnel, the sides of which dissolved the material world into dimness: feelings forced their way through and took over, everything was coloured by emotion. She turned over on her side and no longer breathed regularly, no longer removed the mask when the great waves of pain withdrew, but lay there screaming at the top of her lungs until she had no more air left in her, then she drew a new breath and screamed again, a scream that, though it was partly swallowed up by the mask, was still piercing, unlike anything I had ever heard. Shortly after you tumbled out onto the bed. You were purplish, the thick umbilical cord almost completely blue. Your head was compressed and glistening, your face wrinkled, your eyes closed. You lay perfectly still. You're dead, I thought. Three midwives came running, they rubbed your slippery little body, and you screamed for the first time. It was a feeble scream, more than anything it sounded like the bleating of a lamb.

Up until that moment nothing and no one had been able to reach you, you had lain surrounded by water in the middle of another body, and for a few seconds you remained untouched in the world, lying there as if dead, shut up in yourself, without breathing and with your eyes closed, but then hands reached out to touch you, and you drew your first breath, not without pain, I assume, and the world flowed into you.

FEBRUARY

Hollow Spaces

Much human activity involves creating hollow spaces, that is building walls and floors where before there was nothing, either on a grand scale, as with houses, factory buildings, football stadiums, or smaller versions such as cups, glasses, boxes, tins, coffers, crates, mugs, jars, tanks, vases, bags, satchels, buckets. The hollow spaces are used to store or to transport living beings, objects or liquids. The largest cavities, the houses, are usually stationary, while smaller ones are most often mobile, yet so many gradations in the size and function of cavities exist that even between the stationary house and the mobile vehicle there are intermediate objects such as the caravan or the mobile home. The large cavities are rarely uniform, more often they form complex systems of cavities within cavities. The space created by the four walls, floor and ceiling of a house is in turn subdivided by walls, floors and ceilings, and in the rooms created by these subdivisions, for instance the kitchen, there are new cavities such as cupboards, and within them still more cavities, for instance cups. While stationary cavities are usually considered more grand the larger they are – a palace is grander than a cottage, a large football stadium is grander than a small one – with mobile cavities it is often the other way around: here the smaller the better is the rule. A small cup is finer than a large mug, but a large mug is finer than a bucket. And the very finest objects in a house are stored in tiny jewellery boxes. The urge and the need to create hollows run deep and are not specific to humans. Birds build nests, foxes, badgers and bears make lairs, otters build dens, ants construct mounds, some bees dwell in hollow tree trunks, others build hives, moray eels hide in little grottos within coral reefs, certain crustaceans protect their soft bodies by crawling into empty shells. But humans are the only animal that makes use of mobile cavities. A monkey can form a bowl with its hands, dip it into the water and drink from it, but as soon as it pulls its hands apart, the bowl ceases to exist. When humans learned how to create mobile cavities, they were no longer subject to the constraints of the landscape, but were freed from them: in order to drink, they no longer needed to stay at the source but could transport the water away from it in jars or leather sacks and drink it when they wanted, where they wanted. But this new freedom was double-edged, for whereas before they had lived their lives in the open, they now began living within enclosures, which have since come to dominate our existence completely. Now we live our lives within cavities, and if we leave one by exiting the house, it is only to enter another, the car, which transports us to a third cavity, the office, and from there we stop at the supermarket before returning to the house, with a plastic cavity dangling from each hand, which in turn is filled with cavities filled with food, which we store in the cavities of the house, the fridge, the cupboard. Even when we realise our great dream of leaving earth, we do so in a capsule not much bigger than a car, while the images of earth sent back from it show a perfectly round, blue sphere where not a single one of all these billions of cavities is visible. But they exist, and they mould us more than anything else, for the brain we think with is also contained in a cavity, and all the thoughts we produce are organised like clothes in a wardrobe, with trousers on one shelf, sweaters on another, and the shirts and the dresses hanging on clothes hangers on a rail that stretches from one wall to the other.

Conversation

A great deal of interpersonal communication takes place outside language. If one records a conversation and writes down what was said, it becomes clear how important context is to what is spoken, which in itself is incomplete, characterised by hesitation, lacunae and allusions, and not seldom borders on the meaningless. This is so not only because we employ our whole body to complement our words when we speak, or because in a conversation we are attentive to everything the other bodies convey soundlessly, but because the conversation itself is usually about something quite other than what the words express. A conversation about something that has intrinsic value, where what is said is both important and interesting in itself, occurs so rarely that it clearly isn't the main objective of human intercourse. 'It sure is raining outside' is a fairly common statement, and clearly perfectly meaningless since everyone who hears it can see the rain for themselves. 'It certainly is' might be the equally meaningless reply. Then there might be a pause before the next statement is uttered. 'They say it'll improve a little tomorrow.' What this conversation is really about is impossible to determine until we know where and when it took place, who took part in it and what kind of relationship there was between them. If it occurs in a large house the morning after a party, most guests having left to visit the small coastal town nearby, between two people who have chosen to stay and take it easy, maybe read a little, and who don't know each other but are now in the same room, and he is looking out of the window at the shiny wet green lawn and the heavy grey sky, where dense streaks of rain hang like a gently wavering curtain, and she, who was in a chair reading until he entered the room, but has now risen, walked over to the large tiled stove and put a couple of logs into it, and who, as he says that tomorrow's forecast is better, tears off a piece of newspaper and pushes it in beneath the logs, then the exchange of words about the rain might be a way of establishing a shared space, of affirming that though they don't really know each other, they aren't strangers either, since they have common friends and are now here together. In that case they will each soon go their own way, and before long both the conversation and the situation will be permanently forgotten. But if their eyes met several times during the party the evening before, without any words being exchanged, just these crossed glances, then the conversation in the living room, where she is now striking a match against the rough edge of the big matchbox, and he turns to look at her, and she feels his gaze even though she is crouching with her back to him and poking the lit match into the paper, which immediately catches fire and starts to burn with a thin flame, then it might mean something very different. When she tosses the still-lit match into the fire and stands up, unconsciously rubbing her palms up and down along her thighs as she meets his gaze, and he smiles quietly as he cups the hand that is hanging at his side, and she says, 'But it's good for the farmers at least,' it is turning into a conversation neither of them wants to end, because they are in the process of finding each other through it, and if they do, then perhaps her line 'But it's good for the farmers at least' will later become a classic in their personal mythology, when the first time they met has been turned into a story they remind each other and perhaps also the children of once in a while, to strengthen the bonds that ineluctably weaken over time, and conversations that on paper look flat finally carry no other charge, expressing only indifference.

The Local

When I woke up this morning the ground was covered with hoar frost, and all the little puddles that had formed after the rain of the past few days had frozen, they lay on the stone path like pieces of glass, with frayed white edges. When the sun rose, the landscape glittered as if strewn with precious stones. It stayed cold throughout the day, and the fields and meadows I drove through on my way to school to pick up the children looked transformed, the waterlogged landscape that had seemed to absorb the colours, allowing only a little wilted yellow and some pale green to appear amid the heavy browns, was now sharp and clear, and the frost that lay in fuzzy layers on every straw and branch flashed and sparkled beneath the clear blue sky. Before I came in here I stopped in the garden and stared up into the darkness, which was perforated by the light of myriad stars. I thought about what I imagine everyone thinks about as they gaze out at the universe on a starry winter's night. There are infinite suns out there, and billions of planets orbiting them, and on some of these surely there must be life? Thinking about the universe is often an exercise in abstraction – if one pictures one of its planets it is usually from the outside, as in the images one has seen of the planets of our own solar system, seemingly suspended in empty black space, their shapes and colours not unlike marbles. The first time I saw photographs of a planet taken at ground level, I was shaken. The photos were from Mars, they showed a plain of sand and rock extending towards a mountain that towered up in the distance, the light pale grey as it is on certain autumn mornings. What was so astounding about it? I suddenly realised that it was a place, as concrete and physically real as the frost-covered garden where I have just been standing, gazing at the sky. I understood that it was local. That the spirit of place, what the Romans called *genius loci*, existed there too. And perhaps that is how we should imagine the universe, not as something alien and abstract, all those dizzying numbers and vast distances, but as something nearby and familiar. The wind whipping up a snowdrift beneath an outcrop somewhere in the Pleiades, the air full of swirling snowflakes which in the faint gleam of the moon resemble veils, and the sound of the wind forcing its way through the gulch, wailing, almost whining. A door banging in a house on a desert-like plain near Achernar, a circular lake in a forest on the outskirts of Castor. It is a pleasing thought. And yet it would be a terrible thing if there was life out there and it wasn't like ours but utterly superior, creatures that knew something we didn't, who when they came here threw the doors of the cosmos wide open. All our art, our science, our philosophy, every attempt to understand ourselves and our world, would have lost all meaning overnight. As I write this, it strikes me that that is exactly how it once was. Only a few hundred years ago people were convinced of the existence of a superior power which knew and governed everything and which wasn't human. From the vantage point of this power, the human realm was small, insignificant, invalid and worthless. No human being thought itself capable of comprehending the mystery, and no human striving had human life as its ultimate goal, since art as well as science and philosophy existed solely to serve this higher power. Their humility was boundless, and whoever asserted his own worth, or its specifically human value, was burned at the stake. I don't know what is more frightening: a creature on a small planet worshipping itself and its world as if infinity did not exist, or a creature who burns its fellow beings because the infinite does exist.

Q-tips

Q-tips are little sticks with a cotton-wool swab at each end. They look rather like miniature drum-majorette batons or tiny kayak paddles. Q-tips are usually used to clean the outer ear; one pushes one end into the ear, turns it lightly, and when one pulls it out again, the yellow-brown earwax has stuck to the white cotton wool. Then one does the same with the other ear, using the other end of the Q-tip. Q-tips can also be employed to clean a newborn infant's navel before the decomposing and foul-smelling umbilical stump drops off. Then one moistens the cotton swab with water to reduce friction and in order for the moisture to dissolve the dirt that has gathered there. There is something faintly pleasurable about a box of Q-tips, at least for me; if I happen to catch sight of it in the bathroom cupboard, I nearly always take a Q-tip out and stick it into my ear. The pleasure lies not so much in the touch, the cotton swab is blunt and dry and often feels uncomfortable against the skin inside the ear, especially if one is careless and thrusts it against the eardrum. The scratching noise that fills the skull isn't very agreeable, either. But none of this happens if there is a lot of earwax inside the ear, the wax cancels out the dryness and softens the sound, or changes it from muffled to slightly sticky, and the body is filled with satisfaction, which increases when one removes the cotton swab and finds it covered in a dark tacky layer of earwax. Why this feels so good that I feel a faint tingle of desire every time I see a box of Q-tips, I have no idea. But the urge to remove earwax is related to other insignificant yet real and recurring urges, such as the urge to cut or tear off one's toenails, squeeze blackheads, extract splinters from one's fingers or toes, drain the pus from an infected nail root. At times I get an expectant feeling, a sense that something good is about to happen without remembering exactly what, until it suddenly comes back to me on a wave of disappointment: the good thing I was looking forward to was just cleaning the earwax out of my ear. But I do it anyway, and the time it takes is a pleasurable time. Though Q-tips are common, being found in nearly every home, they are rarely mentioned. Nor are there any instructions for use on the box, so faced with a Q-tip one is left to one's own devices. As I write this, it strikes me that I have never seen anyone else using them. Nor has anyone told me what they are for or given me any form of instruction. Maybe they are intended for entirely different uses? Maybe I have misunderstood completely, and you who are reading this now are sitting there laughing at me? Hey, listen to this! He uses Q-tips to dig earwax out of his ears! That is always the danger in writing about intimate matters, you might be laughed at, and few things are more threatening to a writer than that. In the bathroom one can lock the door and ensure that one is all alone when taking care of intimate business. If it is ridiculous it doesn't matter, no one will ever know. And one of the good things about self-grooming – getting the dirt out of blocked pores, plucking the longest hairs from the mucous membrane in the nose, trimming one's eyebrows – is precisely that one isn't being observed or judged by anyone, not even by oneself, one simply stands there vacantly in front of the mirror, filled with the calm of self-maintenance. It may be that humans will one day be surpassed by computers and robots, that artificial intelligence will develop both agency and self-consciousness, but it will never develop either earwax or Q-tips, nose hair or nose clippers, and as long as that remains the case, as long as we are the only beings able to find peace in manicures, we will do perfectly fine.

This morning we drove to the local pastry shop, Olof Viktor's, to have lunch. They don't serve hot meals but are known for their excellent bread, and beneath the glass counter there were open sandwiches with few but fancy toppings: a mountain of crayfish tails piled on some, thick slices of brie stacked on top of various vegetables on others. I wanted something with meat in it and bent over to read the little sign posted between those sandwiches that had layers of meat on them. The meat was white, it could have been chicken or turkey, or maybe even slices of beef. But the sign said '*tupp*', Swedish for 'rooster'. I felt disgusted, and when I righted myself, my appetite was gone. Why didn't I want to eat rooster? I have no problem eating chicken or cooked hen, for instance in a casserole, but I felt an instinctive reaction against rooster. I ordered a brie sandwich instead and tried to think of something else as we sat down in the large, almost empty room, big enough to hold the hordes of people who come here in the summer. The fields beyond the windows were covered by a thin layer of snow, with the brown soil showing through in places, as when a wound is visible through strips of gauze. It must be because the rooster has such a distinct identity that it stands out,

I thought. The rooster is stately, unlike the short and nearly rotund hens, and it cranes its neck as it struts around as if to survey the scene, turning its head here and there with jerky and staccato movements. This gives the rooster a highly strung air, as if it were constantly on the verge of exploding into movement, which must be why it was a symbol of vigilance in antiquity. The rooster enjoys every privilege in the chicken coop: at night it roosts on the best perch, at the very top, and it is allowed to impregnate the hens and thus perpetuate its genes. But this comes at a price, for the rooster's task is also to protect the flock from attackers, and it is granted its privileges only by virtue of being the strongest, a position challenged by the younger cocks, who attack as soon as they feel strong enough. Such cockfights are brutal and bloody spectacles, for the rooster is inherently single-minded, so when it goes on the attack, there is nothing beyond the desire to harm and kill. The red cockscomb shares something of the triumphant aura of the warrior's helmet plume and may in fact have inspired it; in antiquity the rooster was also a symbol of belligerence. And the cockscomb doesn't resemble only the plume, for it widens and covers the rooster's head around the eyes like a helmet, before ending in two bag-like protuberances that dangle beneath its beak. But although these human-like attributes may make it hard to eat rooster, at least not as unreluctantly as other kinds of meat, they don't make it impossible. In the car on the way home, passing the wide, slumbering fields, it struck me that there is also something underworldly about the rooster. Something underworldly? Where did that come from? It had something to do with a poem by the Norwegian poet Olav H. Hauge. When we got home, I skimmed the table of contents of my edition of his collected poems. There I found 'The Gold Rooster', which opens like this:

And I was dead a long time. Dead inside my shell,
and I crowed like the golden cock of Constantinople.
I lived beneath – I heard grating sounds and an answer –
and fought against – and the cry of the betrayed soul
sounded hollow.

The rooster in the poem is an enigmatic figure, evoking external pomp, even tawdry ostentation, but also death and that which lies beneath. Miklagard, the Old Norse name for Constantinople, made me think of the Vikings. There was also something familiar about the first sentence. 'And I was dead a long time.' It is a fantastic line, one of the greatest ever in Norwegian poetry. But I had read it somewhere else only a few weeks ago. I vaguely associated it with the Vikings too, and got out the *Eddic Poems*. In 'Baldr's Dreams' I found it. There, the Volva says 'long was I dead'. The Volva is in the underworld, and Odin has woken her from the dead to find out the meaning of Baldr's bad dreams. In the land of the dead the tables have been laid for a magnificent feast; it is Baldr they are expecting. So Hauge's line was taken from an Eddic poem, but in it there were no roosters, so where did the rooster's association with the underworld come from? Was it Hauge's own? Something told me that it wasn't, so I continued leafing through the book and was soon completely engrossed in these beautiful

old poems. Late in the afternoon, when it had begun snowing again, I found the Norse rooster. It was in 'Voluspo', in
the following lines:

> *Above him the cock*
> *in the bird-wood crowed,*
> *Fair and red*
> *did Fjalar stand.*
> *Then to the gods*
> *crowed Gollinkambi,*
> *He wakes the heroes*
> *in Odin's hall;*
> *And beneath the earth*
> *does another crow,*
> *The rust-red bird*
> *at the bars of Hel.*

Was it the underworldly rooster, the cock that crows
beneath the earth, that had prevented me from buying the
undoubtedly tasty sandwiches at the pastry shop? I would
never know, impulses are rarely linked to thoughts, there is
no congruity between a feeling of disgust and a psychological explanation for it. Nevertheless, it had lain there
all the time like an undertone, a different and darker
chord beneath the cheerful *'tupp'* and 'rooster' of my consciousness. And once I had identified the chord, another
association surfaced with it: my grandmother's sister,
Borghild Larsen, who lived in Årdal in Jølster, in a little
house just above the place where she was born and grew up,
once told me as we were sitting on her veranda looking out
at the wide, gentle Jølstravatnet lake, that when someone

drowned there in the old days they used a rooster to locate the body. They put the rooster on board the boat, rowed slowly across the lake, and where the rooster crowed, they stopped and dredged for the dead.

Fish

When you are fishing from a smooth rock slope and there is a nibble and you reel in a fish, which a few minutes later is thrashing about on shore, it is striking how the even, polished surface of the rock, where nothing stands out and there are no rough, grooved or in other ways irregular edges or ridges, is seemingly repeated in the body of the fish, which also appears polished, with its gently curving streamlined shape which begins at the root of the tail, and on the upper side rises towards the back before subsiding towards the mouth, while on the lower side it traces the same rising and falling curve along the belly, so that the body of the fish is closed like an ellipse, and compared to land animals, with the exception of snakes and serpents, is merely a torso. If one imagines what it is like to be a fish, it is hard not to feel the urge to stretch out one's arms and touch what one sees and a sense of despair when this isn't possible. The fish feels neither urge nor despair, it lacks for nothing as, searching for something to eat, it glides over the seabed with wave-like movements which travel through its body. That this armless existence, where everything gripped is gripped with the mouth, developed at an earlier stage than ours, and that arms can therefore be seen as an add-on, a kind of accessory which regardless of how crucial they seem to living a full life on land are not strictly necessary, lends the arms a slightly showy air as we bend over the fish and extract the hook from its mouth with one hand while grasping its body with the other, a body that feels smooth and cold but still full of life and vigour, which ceases abruptly in a dark explosion when we smash its head against the rock and the fish dies.

I grew up on an island, yet the life I related to, which I occasionally caught a glimpse of and which we learned about in school, was that of plants, trees, land animals and birds. Badger, fox, crow, spruce, birch, sparrow, raven, deer, adder, moose, gull, wood anemone, frog, bluebell, grass snake, ash, oak, squirrel, foxglove, horsetail, moss, hare, pine. Not that life in the surrounding ocean was forgotten, it just didn't belong to the world I identified with and felt a part of, but to a wholly other world, on the other side as it were, almost like the starry sky, only closer and therefore more neutral. To drop the sinker over the side and feel it rushing down into the deep beneath the boat until it hit the bottom with a sudden weightlessness and had to be reeled in a little to hang suspended like a probe from the world of air, with a row of metal hooks above it that the fish, in their slow ocean-current rhythm were supposed to nibble, was of course exciting, but in a mechanical way – would they take the bait? – not unlike the longing for a goal in a football match, and had nothing of the crackling mystery of the starry sky. Not even when the fish struck and became visible in the water beneath the boat like silvery flashes. The first time this happened was the summer I was thirteen, and I suddenly understood, with all the force of an obvious insight, that the islets in the archipelago were really mountaintops, and that the sea belonged to the landscape, it flowed onto the land, covering the low-lying areas and forming canals between the elevations, so that the fish swam between the mountains down there just as the birds flew between the mountains up here. This thought suddenly drew fish into the world and placed the mackerel on an equal footing with the magpie, the cod with the beaver, the flounder with the hedgehog, the ling with the swallow. Slowly they swam around in their valleys, through their sub-aquatic forests, over their open plains towards the towering mountainsides, where some of them, especially cod, liked to pause in the wintertime, while my father, only a few metres above them, cast his lures out over the water, with me looking on, while the waves crashed and shattered against the rock below us and filled the air with drops of saltwater, which the powerful onshore wind swept inland, so that our hair was stiff when we got home later that day, with our bucket full of smooth cold fish beating their tails though they were long since dead.

Winter Boots

Over the years I must have had something like thirty pairs of winter boots, and I must have worn them every day during the entire winter, sometimes for two winters, and yet I can barely remember a single pair. This is precisely because they were used so often and with such familiarity: everyday life makes things disappear, the everyday is like a zone where whatever lands within is doomed to oblivion. In addition, boots belong to the zeitgeist, that invisible nexus which links all people and inspires them to design objects that resemble each other, and since things that look the same are harder both to see and to remember than things that look different, it is as if a shadow lies across most of our possessions and clothing, which only the most distinctive among them are able to penetrate. These, on the other hand, can glow in our consciousness over a span of several decades. When it comes to winter boots, a pair that I remember well is typically one that I didn't get. They were so-called Sami boots, tall, snug-fitting around the calves, of light-coloured leather, with upturned toes. Why I wanted them so badly I have no idea, but I did, I have a memory of standing in front of the display window of the shoe shop in Arendal staring at the fabled boots. It may have been due to a TV series that was shown around that time, about a Sami boy called Ante, which had a big influence on me and everyone I knew. My mother knitted me a sweater that I thought of as Sami-like, it had split sides so that the front and back panels flapped loosely, not unlike the loincloths I had seen American Indians wear, and American Indian was the other association woken by both the sweater and the boots, via the Sami. Once when I was running down the hill towards the house wearing the sweater, I remember having a distinct 'Sami feeling', I was like a Sami or an American Indian, and the feeling filled me with jubilation. That instant, which can't have lasted more than a few seconds, is one of my strongest childhood memories. The wind in my face, the loincloth-like flaps slapping against my thighs and bum as I ran, the gravel crunching under my feet, the fog hanging between the trees on the other side of the road. I suppose it was that feeling I wanted to have again as I stood staring at the tall light-coloured boots in the shop window. Besides, they looked really nice. Back then I thought that nice-looking clothes, shoes and boots would make me look nice, or beautiful as I would say now. That looking nice, or beautiful, wasn't anything to aspire to I didn't learn until a few years later, when the same boots became something I wouldn't have been caught dead wearing.

Of all the boots I have actually owned, not just wanted to own, there is a pair I remember. Not because they were either particularly nice or particularly warm. On the contrary, they were old and cracked, I had inherited them from my brother, they had holes, and the soles were worn thin. They were low with a zipper on the side. They were black, but the black had worn away at the tips, where they were grey. My socks got wet in those boots, and my feet were always cold. I wasn't allowed to wear them to school, so I took them in a plastic bag in my backpack and changed into them as soon as I was on the bus. I did this because the boots had a unique property: the soles were worn so smooth that there was hardly any friction between them and the snow. And this was a winter when a new fad had appeared, one of many that spread like wildfire and for a few weeks dominated our activities at the housing development and in the school playground. Instead of setting off down the steepest slopes on skis, plastic sledges, kicksleds, toboggans or wooden sledges with steering wheels, we skidded down on our boots. That was the big thing. When the snowplough had been, the snow on the slopes was sometimes smooth as ice, shining like mirrors in the glare of the street lights, and then it was possible to slide even on boots that were brand new and had deep, grooved patterns on their soles. If conditions were less ideal, only worn-out soles without grooves did the trick. This made my old, tattered, almost Chaplinesque boots hugely valuable. With them on my feet I could slide down any slope in nearly any weather conditions and reach extremely high speeds. We became good at it: in the evenings, in the yellow light of the street lamps, one could see three or four skinny boys whizzing down the hill on their boots, some leaning forward like downhill skiers, others standing bolt upright, as if this wasn't happening and they were really in a very different situation, talking to someone at a crossroads, say, while others again swayed and tottered like walking pipe cleaners. But none slid faster than me, thanks to my magic boots which fate had so unexpectedly bestowed on me. And if I equate the child I was then with the man I am now and say that the child's happiness is worth every bit as much as the man's, then those weeks were probably the happiest of my life: it is the only time I have achieved everything I dreamed of.

Feeling of Life

We invariably feel something, and we are always in a certain mood. But although our feelings and moods dominate our existence in such a fundamental way, no one knows precisely what they are, where they originate, what they consist of, why they are there. Through experiments neurologists have managed to localise certain types of thoughts and cognitive activities in certain parts of the brain, but feelings and moods are not thoughts, they have no specific location, they are more like the backdrop to our thoughts. Nor do feelings and moods appear to be a part of the conscious self, for while they are continually changing, the self observes the change and in a sense stands aloof from it, even though emotions and moods sometimes take over and dominate it entirely, as for instance in an uncontrolled rage, overpowering joy or depression. But if it is true that the self is not identical to its feelings and moods, then it should be possible to imagine a self that feels nothing and is never in a given mood. Yet there is no such neutral self. Perhaps the relationship is reflected in the way we speak about it when we say that someone is highly or lowly strung, in other words that emotions and moods influence the self in the same way that the tuning of an instrument influences the music it produces.

That the instrument corresponds to the thoughts, the key to the emotions and the mood, the music to the self, and that what is realised through the music is the soul. All analogies linking the inner life to exterior phenomena and objects not only reduce it, but also connect it to the age, such as for instance seventeenth-century notions about the brain as a kind of machine or clock, or our present notions of the brain as a computer with software, hardware and memory. Music is the only other thing I know of which, like the soul, originates in something technical and material, in the case of musical instruments in strings and screws, pipes and hollow spaces, plates and bows, in the case of the soul in nerve fibres, membranes, axons and dendrites, without the product of the material starting point ever being in any way traceable back to it. Mapping the brain's functions is like studying the work of an instrument maker in his workshop, analysing the age and origin of the wood, its humidity and elasticity, and the chemical composition of the strings or the glue in order to explain a symphony. But the differences are of course greater than the similarities, not least because music is composed, that is to say formed by a will, while all our various moods, which stream through our consciousness every day, are not shaped by will but simply arise within us. Not arbitrarily, they are tuned to what we have seen and experienced, how we were created and what we have become, but they are still beyond our control. I didn't choose to wake up every morning feeling dejected, and though I know what causes it, that the inner self circles around itself and doesn't allow enough room for the external world, there's nothing I can do about it. But that shutting out the world influences feelings and moods and that it represents a distortion of the original state of human existence, this is something I know, both because I have children and see how the world flows through them and because I myself have been a child and remember what it was like, but also because on a very few occasions I have experienced everything within me lifting and becoming light and easy, and each time it was caused by a powerful experience of the world. The experience of art can be powerful too, it can lift one up and seem light but without leaving what it is bound to – as when a branch is lifted by the wind, when all its leaves tremble and flicker and are filled with glinting reflections of sunlight. The lightness of experiencing the world is different, it isn't centred on anything in particular, what fills the soul is precisely the lightness of the indefinite. Not the branch lifting in the wind, but the wind. Not the leaves reflecting the sunlight, but the sunlight.

J.

The last time I saw J. was a couple of days ago, I drove past his house and saw him sitting in a deckchair by the wall, asleep and wrapped in woollen blankets. His mouth was open, and he is so thin now that at a distance his gaping head looked almost like a skull. J. has always been small and slight, but the force within him has been such that I haven't given that a thought, not until the last two or three years, during which his illness has both crippled his fingers, which now resemble those of a witch, and given him a stoop, while his enormous energy is gone completely. He looked like a small bundle lying there in the chair. Perhaps the most characteristic thing about J. now is that time, which has so ravaged his body, has left his soul in peace. His face is wrinkled and creased, and his body is twisted, not unlike the trees by the sea forced by all the storms and tempests to grow at the most baroque angles, but his soul is apparently wholly untouched, it seems as pure and untainted by experience as it must have been when he was seven years old. He is now sixty-six. His eyes are mischievous, full of amusement but also self-conscious, for J. has obvious narcissistic traits. His self-consciousness, however, doesn't seem to apply to who he is, only to who he happens to be in a given situation, and therefore has to do with his charm. A couple of years ago, when he wasn't as enfeebled as he is now, I would sometimes run into him at the local restaurant, and there was something impressive about the figure he cut then, he had a full beard, and his deeply lined face might have belonged to one of the Bible's patriarchs. He radiated dignity, but in a wild way, typical of a wilful person, not entirely unlike the wildness peculiar to old age that the older Beckett emanates in photos. But when I stopped in front of his table or sat down at it, and he began to speak, it was as if the grimly ravaged face didn't really belong to him but was a kind of mask that his gentle eyes had put to use and shaped into the facial expressions of his childish impulses. I experienced this several times, and though I partly recognised it, since my maternal grandfather had had something of the same air about him, it was different; I had seen it in glimpses in my grandfather, when whatever held his old man's dignity together cracked, but in J.'s character there were clearly no such unifying elements. What held him together? J. approached everyone as if they were children because he himself was like a child, and no one had ever corrected this, nor had he allowed himself to be corrected: all his life J. has been a celebrated figure.

About a year later I was invited to a party in his garden. It was in the spring, the light of the low-lying sun flowed over the tables that had been placed out on the lawn and the festively dressed people who sat around them. I had brought one of my daughters with me, she was eight and excited about meeting the host, whom I had told her about. But he wasn't there. Two men came out of the house carrying food and placed it on a table already laden with bottles of beer and wine and soft drinks. One of them said in a loud voice that J. would be coming out soon and had said we should just start eating. So we did. When is he coming? my daughter asked several times during the meal. When is J. coming?

When he finally arrived, supported by the same two men who had carried out the food, her eyes widened. His tiny, thin, slumped body was dressed all in white, and his jacket, which was wide and reached almost to his knees, might have belonged to a maharaja. On his white breast he bore a conspicuous medal, a decoration awarded by the King for meritorious service, over his mouth he wore a narrow moustache, his eyes were hidden behind a pair of sunglasses, and his hair was slicked back smoothly. He stopped, the two men stepped away, and with his chest puffed up he gazed out over the assembled guests. He looked like a South American dictator. He said a few words, then sat down at our table. One of the men poured vodka into a glass, which he swallowed in one gulp, breathing heavily. For the next half-hour he spoke uninterruptedly about himself and his affairs. My daughter didn't take her eyes off him. Finally she gathered up enough courage to ask him a question. Then it was as if he laid everything else aside, he leaned forward towards her, asked her to repeat her question and remained in that position, with his entire attention focused on her, as if only she existed, for at least ten minutes.

She was spellbound. Even without having heard him sing. For that is J.'s most prominent attribute, the great voice which no one would believe could issue from his tiny body, which has made him what he is and led him to where he is now, lying with his mouth gaping open in front of the house on his manor-like estate in the cold glare of the February sun, apparently dying.

Buses

It has been snowing for two days, and this morning I heard that the school bus service has been cancelled. The snow cover is fairly thin, and it seems excessively cautious to cancel the bus and keep children from attending school because of it. Typically Swedish, I thought, and remembered a time in Malmö when people were asked to stay indoors and not venture out unless absolutely necessary, a storm was coming. The storm came, and I took the children outside to look at it, we walked through the deserted streets while the wind rumpled our hair and overturned the occasional traffic sign. There was no danger, it was just windy, the authorities' directive was hysterical. And now they didn't dare drive the children to school because of a few centimetres of freshly fallen snow. I told Geir A. on the phone, thinking we might share a laugh at Sweden's expense as we used to do, but he didn't think it had anything to do with either caution or cowardice, but rather with finance. They're saving money, none of the buses here have snow chains, haven't you noticed? I hadn't. It had been several years since I even thought about snow chains. Suddenly it came back to me, the phenomenon that filled the roads with its beautiful, rhythmic clanking during the 70s, when all buses, lorries and many private vehicles had metal chains fitted over their tyres when it snowed. Back then buses were almost like boxes, they had few of today's aerodynamic curves, which make buses look a little like boats, gently rolling cruise ships rearing up above the cars on busy roads. They were different on the inside too, for while today's buses, with their comfortable seats and elaborate interiors, often in dark colours, resemble living rooms, the interiors of buses back then were more like outhouses or sheds. And while today's buses are quiet, then they were filled with the rumbling drone of their engines, which made everything rattle and shake, floors, windows, seats, as if we, fighting our way into them from the blizzard outside with our school bags swinging from our shoulders, were entering a kind of assembly plant. That this shed-like box, almost like a workshop on wheels, could allow itself to be obstructed by something as plain as snow was unthinkable. It did slow down a bit going uphill, but that was all. The 70s were the last robust decade. Why the decades that followed became more and more finely tuned is difficult to say, but it may simply have been that the tender souls of the 70s, the ones who sat pale and feminine in their seats staring out at the snow-covered landscape and dreaming of being far away from the roaring engines, the rattling seats and the jeering boys – who on days like this spent their afternoons outside the shop, and as soon as the drivers got into their seats, ran bent double towards the cars, crouched behind them and remained there, holding on tight to the rear bumpers while the cars drove out of the parking lot and down the road, sliding on their shoes and competing to see who dared to hang on the longest, a competition that also included the buses, which were so wide that there was room for four or five crouching boys dragged along behind towards the main road, where they dropped off one after the other, not unlike the rhythm of paratroopers jumping out of a plane, and slowly lost speed until they came to a stop and lay motionless in the road for a few seconds, probably laughing, before they jumped up again and ran back to find another vehicle to hang on to – those who were unable to take part in this or any other of the games of that time and were made anxious by the brutal noise and look of the many snowploughs, that these delicate dreamers, fine-tuned as clocks, were far more numerous than anyone could have imagined.

Habits

For some reason writers are often asked about their routines and habits, such as what time they get up to write, whether they write by hand or on a computer, whether there is something they can't do without while they are writing. What it is about the writer's role in particular that awakens public interest in their daily lives is hard to say, but there must be something, since this doesn't happen with other comparable professions. Maybe it has to do with the fact that everyone can write and read while at the same time there is something exalted about the role of the writer, and that this gap, which seems incomprehensible, must be bridged. Or it may have to do with the fact that writing is voluntary, and that a person who writes can always refrain from doing so, which is unthinkable in the case of an employee, and therefore obscure or tempting. When I was young I read interviews with writers with avid interest. I wasn't looking for a method, I don't think; what I wanted to find out was rather what it took. A pattern, a common denominator: what makes a writer a writer? Now I know that all writers are amateurs, and that perhaps the only thing they have in common is that they don't know how a novel, a short story or a poem should be written. This fundamental uncertainty creates the need for habits, which are nothing other than a framework, scaffolding around the unpredictable. Children need the same thing, something has to be repeated in their lives, and this can't be something inner, it has to involve external reality, they must know in advance at least some of what is happening around them. That repetition is not innate to us, the way it is to most other beings, but has to be created and maintained by acts of will, is perhaps the main difference between animals and humans. Animals such as dogs who are taken from their natural surroundings and introduced into new settings have nothing to parry unpredictability with, and get caught up in insane repetitions, tics and other compulsive acts. If it is great enough, children react to unpredictability in similar ways. Anxiety, aggression, antisocial behaviour. Dante held that we can never understand the actions or feelings of others by reference to our own, as the baser animals can, and that this is why God gave us language. In other words, to make the differences visible, so that they become predictable and functional and enable social relations. But if differences are repeated, they become similarities, that is their own opposite. This makes language treacherous, it serves two masters, and that and no other is the reason literature exists. And that is why only people who are unable to write are able to write it. For if habit is allowed into literature and not kept outside, it is no longer literature, merely still more scaffolding around life.

The Brain

The brain, which in an adult human being weighs well over a kilo, consists of two symmetrical hemispheres separated by a fissure running lengthwise, and resembles most of all a large walnut, also in that the surface appears coiled, full of folds and depressions, and that like the walnut the brain is encased in a hard, round, box-like shell. But while the walnut is dry, shrunken and lifeless, the brain is moist, with liquids flowing through it, and in that respect is closer to a clam, which also consists of a soft living interior enclosed in a protective shell. The crucial difference is of course that the clam is a single entity, a separate being, while the brain is merely one organ of a greater whole, namely the human body, with which the brain connects through the many nerve threads leading out of it. But if one could remove the brain from the cranium and extricate each and every one of these threads which run from the brain down through the neck and out into every part of the body, the brain would look like a separate creature, not one of the land animals, since it would lack arms and legs, but one of those that drift along in the ocean. With the nerve threads trailing behind it like a veil, the brain would be not unlike a jellyfish. It would have its pale grey-white colours in common with other beings that live in places where daylight never reaches, also its blindness. In these circumstances one must imagine that brains would develop little mouths, perhaps beneath the frontal lobes, and a basic digestive system with soft narrow intestines running through the folds, maybe also a small gut or pyloric stomach on the underside. Since they would be relatively heavy and compact, and would have neither the soft matter nor the flexible disc shape of jellyfish, they would be forced to seek out places on the seabed where there was movement in the water, currents strong enough that plankton and krill or other tiny ocean creatures drifted past them and could be snatched up with their little mouths, or perhaps with their long thin nerve threads, the electricity in which would be sufficient to stun slightly larger creatures, and which they would perhaps have learned how to move so that their prey could be transported to the mouth. It isn't hard to imagine brains like this, lying motionless on the seabed like small boulders in gatherings of a hundred, maybe a hundred and fifty, with veils of nerves wafting dully back and forth above them. Occasionally, when the current was strong, some on the periphery would come loose and drift slowly along, bobbing like leather balls in the water, before coming to rest in a new place. What they would be thinking as they lay there is anyone's guess, but it is reasonable to suppose that they would develop further the Buddhist potential that all brains have. They would cultivate the insight that the world is an illusion, seeking the spaces between thoughts as if to rest in the emptiness there, which would increase year after year until finally there would be hardly anything but emptiness within them. The thoughts that would come drifting into this void would be pale and vague, no longer recognisable as thoughts, and when they filled the brains, it would be in a dreamlike way, shining like a street light in the fog. That this is also the shape of fish thoughts they wouldn't know, for they no would longer think in any other way, but merely let themselves be filled with the pale light, which first appeared as a small shining point, growing slowly until it filled them and then began to fade away. The emptiness that followed was not something they reflected upon either, except in so far as there remained in some of them the faintest of expectations of light to come, like a kind of reverberation, until it too faded and they all lay motionless down there in the dark, thinking of nothing.

Sex

When I was growing up, there were two narratives about sex. One came from the porn magazines that began circulating among the boys in the housing development from about the age of ten, where sex was something secret, forbidden, dirty and well-nigh criminal, yet also enticing, since all boundaries were eliminated, we were given glimpses of a completely hedonistic world so unlike the one we knew that we could hardly believe it, while at the same time it was slowly dawning on us that that world also existed here, among our parents and teachers, the people who manned the shops and drove the buses, people we saw on TV and listened to on the radio. The other narrative about sex was exactly the opposite: it was about love, the one great love of one's life whom one would one day marry and have kids with. That story too was present around us in every conceivable form, in books, movies, magazines, comic books and in that part of our parents' lives visible to us. The two narratives were so different that it was impossible to join them into one, even though they dealt with the same thing. This irreconcilability dominated how I related to sex back then, when I was growing up, and it still does. Ever since I was a child I have regarded the feminine as something exalted and unattainable, both admiring and desiring the world of women, which was so filled with beauty, from the clothes found in it, with all their details and refinements, to the ambivalent smiles, sometimes warm and teasing, sometimes cold and dismissive, from the thin wrists to the rounded, soft shapes, the curve of the hips and the swell of the breasts, to the neat, refined movements. I wanted all of this, I wanted to be part of it, I wanted to wallow in it. But since I considered first all girls and then all women to be far more worthy than myself, even completely superior, there was no way to enter their world. The only girls and later women I could talk to were the ones I respected as little as I respected myself, those who weren't particularly attractive and whom I didn't desire. If, contrary to expectation, late one evening I successfully contrived to be alone with a woman I admired and wanted, my silence and the nearly all-encompassing importance I assigned to the encounter, which must have shone wildly and desperately in my eyes, was so off-putting that it almost never led to anything other than footsteps vanishing down a road, up a staircase, into an apartment. On the rare occasions when it actually did lead to something, my desire after years of intense fantasising was so great that I came almost instantly, so I never got to where I wanted to be, where I could wallow in breasts and thighs, buttocks and wet clefts. Premature ejaculation is of course the telltale sign of the infantile man, but it is also linked to anxiety, fear of the feminine, at least in my case. Once when a girl I was in love with returned my feelings, and we became a couple, I was so afraid of doing the only thing I wanted that I told her I thought we should get to know each other better before we slept together. She looked puzzled but accepted my suggestion. Several weeks passed, and I was permanently panicked. I fear women, and what I fear is that I will be found lacking, that I won't be good enough. The irony, of course, is that it is precisely this fear that causes one to be found lacking, to be not good enough, for the maleness that women desire, at least in my experience, means self-sufficiency, wilfulness, supremacy. But if one gets to the point where the narrative of the one true love merges with the narrative of hedonistic, boundless sex, gradually other obstacles arise, for that kind of sex is contingent on distance, and if one is in a relationship, if one lives together every day, it is in the nature of the relationship that the distance gets smaller and smaller, one grows closer and closer together, that is what we call love, and the greater the love, the more difficult it becomes to reconcile it with sex, unless one is able to turn it into a game, and pretend that the person one is sleeping with doesn't matter. Perhaps that is the supreme act of love, it strikes me now.

Snowdrifts

In Norse mythology Fonn is a *gyger*, a female jotun, the sister of Torre, Mjoll and Driva and the daughter of Snow, who in turn is the son of Jokul. When we know that *fonn* was the Norse word for a large accumulation of snow, that *torre* was hoar frost, *mjoll* a dense snowfall, *driva* a snow flurry and *jokul* ice, then a separate reality emerges, for not only do these names afford us a glimpse of a cold snow-filled world, but also of a belief that its various aspects represented different powers. The boundary between personification and naming is fluid, for even if we don't believe that a blizzard is a supernatural force, it still represents a separate state of nature, creating a space all its own and giving rise to particular moods or tonalities, and through the name all this is delineated and assembled, so that we are able not only to recognise it as something separate when it is present but also to invoke it when it is absent. O snow squall, flurry and sleet! O blizzard, slush and crust! O packing snow, O powder snow, O lovely deep snowdrift! Even in the housing development where I grew up, with its new streets, houses and gardens, the many varieties of snow left their mark on life and the landscape and at times dominated them completely. I remember one winter in particular because of the tremendous amounts of snow that fell, day after day it drifted down, large wet snowflakes from a grey heavy sky. Between the black and motionless trees below the road, their trunks shimmering with moisture, the clustered snowflakes fell, over the lawns, the driveways and the roofs, over the roads, the building sites, the fields, over the floating docks, the bridge and the sound, everywhere the snowflakes fell, so densely that the air was almost completely white. It grew colder and the snow became drier, lighter; now it whirled in the wind, now it swept along the ground, and one could see the paths usually taken by the wind, it was forced up along the brick wall there and channelled into the space between the camper van and the house here, it came rushing out of the forest there and with renewed force flung itself across the open ice-covered space above the narrow bay until it encountered the mountain on the other side and was again forced up. When the wind died down and the snowfall ceased, the landscape was completely transformed. The roads had grown walls, in some places the tall snow banks left by the ploughs made them look like gullies. The forest had a new floor, it was white and pillowy and covered every unevenness in the terrain. At the foot of slopes, before every elevation in the landscape, whether it was the walls of a house, rock outcrops, uprooted trees or the steep bank of a creek, the snow lay in drifts, in some places several metres deep. What could one do with them? One could jump into them. And the jumping spread like wildfire through the housing development. We jumped from every overhang we could find, hesitantly at first, not unlike the hesitation that occurred at new places to dive off when no one quite knew whether the water was deep enough, then eagerly and confidently. First from a height of a couple of metres, then three, four, some going on to five, the wildest maybe even to six metres – dimensions are experienced differently in childhood, a rock can seem a mountain, a glade in the forest a plain, a garage a hangar – but certainly life was rarely more exciting and filled with possibilities as we climbed onto roofs and jumped, climbed up on overhanging rocks and jumped, climbed trees and jumped. The world had opened up, suddenly it contained new opportunities of a fantastic sort, for humans were not meant to fly through the air out in the forest. That only children sought out the fantastic – I never saw a single adult struggle up onto a roof or an overhang to jump into the snowdrift below – seemed odd at the time, but not now, when I myself am an adult and openness towards the new, the leap and its promise of freedom are unwanted. Not merely because it is childish and because there would be something shameful about being seen jumping off the roof by the neighbour, but also because habit, stasis and constraint have become like old friends, I know them so well, I know what they have to offer, and that is more important than either the new, the fall or its freedom.

Vanishing Point

From the window where I am sitting and writing, I look over towards the house we live in. A few minutes ago a man came walking along the stone path, stopped in front of the door and knocked. People rarely come here, other than the parents of our children's friends, so I felt a prick of anxiety even as I guessed that he was working for a delivery service. I got up, went out and called out to him. He had reddish-blond hair, a broad chin, a gaze which registered whatever was going on around him but didn't seem particularly interested in it. Knasgard? he said. I nodded. I have a parcel for you, he said. I followed him over to the lorry that was parked on the road behind the house, he got into the back, it was almost empty and seemed disproportionately large compared to the small box he handed me. I signed with my finger on the portable device he held out, and when I returned to the house I heard the vehicle door slam and the engine start. Afterwards I sat for a while wondering about scale. None of the people who come here, walking along the footpath or across the lawn, are anonymous, they are not just anybody, though they frequently come as representatives of their profession, often delivery drivers but also plumbers, electricians, carpenters, the occasional lottery ticket vendor.

Even though I have never seen them before and know nothing about them, not even their names, they are somebody, particular persons with particular personalities, unlike all others, that is apparent as soon as they enter my field of vision. The way they hold their heads, their way of walking, their inner rhythm, what their faces radiate. To ourselves we are always who we are, while to others the person we are is something that emerges gradually, something that arrives with us and then disappears again. Human beings have a vanishing point, which we move in and out of, a zone where to other people we go from being definite to indefinite, from indefinite to definite. This indefinite person, faceless and devoid of character, lives within patterns which constrain him and provides the material for statistics. Approximately the same number of people die in traffic accidents every year, drown in the ocean and lakes and rivers every summer, pass through the metro turnstiles every January morning, even though that particular traffic accident, that particular drowning, that particular metro ride came about through a series of personal, individual decisions. If you look out over the suburb from your seventeenth-floor apartment one morning that is what you see, how all the people, those black antlike little creatures, follow the same roads and paths, according to a rhythm that none of them is in charge of, first the deluge of people going to work, then the more scattered pattern of those who remain in the area during the day, the elderly, the parents pushing prams, those on sick leave, and then a new flood of people at the end of the working day. These movements can easily be simulated by a computer with only a few variables, for regardless of what we are thinking as we walk across the frozen pond on our way home to our apartment, regardless of how uniquely original our thoughts happen to be as we bend our heads and gaze at the trampled snow, we are simultaneously and always entirely predictable, since we also belong to a greater movement, like a bird in a large flock that suddenly wheels synchronously in the air, where for a moment it resembles an enormous waving hand.

The 1970s

Once in a while I tell my children about the 1970s. Much of it has to do with what we didn't have. No Internet, no mobile phones, no iPads, no Macs or PCs, no ATM machines or credit cards. No car windows that slid down by themselves or car keys that could lock and unlock doors from a distance. Seeing the face of the person you were talking to on the phone was a regular feature of science fiction series then and perhaps the most futuristic image we could imagine. The children are beginning to tire of these stories, since their moral is so obvious: previously every little thing required an effort, like listening to a certain kind of music or withdrawing money from the bank, and the fact that nothing came easy or was free of cost made everything more valuable. The only thing the children hear when I talk like this is that everything was better before. Their dad is sitting in the driver's seat telling them how good everything used to be and how bad everything is now, how spoiled they are, how little they do, how lucky they are. That is to say, in this way of thinking 'lucky' becomes its opposite: when their dad, who loves the 70s so much, tells them they are lucky to have it so easy, what he really means is that they are unlucky, and that the lucky ones are those who have a harder time than them.

It's not good to devalue your children's lives and lifestyles in this way. The children, who in any case will never experience the 70s, contradict me as best they can. They call me an old fogey, the music I play in the car they call Stone Age music. No one likes rock any more, Dad, they say. When I tell them people in the 70s lived in modern times too, they shake their heads, they refuse to accept it, *they* are the ones who are modern. And it isn't so strange: they are as distant from the 70s as I was from the 1930s at their age. In other words, the Peasant Party, Vidkun Quisling, Zeppelins, herring stop seines, the Great Depression, the Model T Ford, the Berlin Olympics. I never heard my father or my mother praise the 1950s, when they grew up, they felt no trace of nostalgia; on the contrary I got the impression they were glad to have put that time behind them. That's why I like the 70s, they were both a part of the past – when eating in a restaurant was something extraordinary, for example, and there were hardly any places to eat out other than the wonderful roadside cafés, when entertainment was suspect, something that had to be rationed out in small portions on TV and the radio, and hay-drying racks could still be seen everywhere in the countryside – and of the future, in that the technology was already in place, only in a rudimentary version, with telephones that were physically connected to a network of cables, TVs and radios that were like big wooden boxes, and rockets that were hardly more advanced than cars, lifting heavily and almost reluctantly from the ground on an enormous plume of fire before they slowly increased their speed and rose higher and higher in the clear blue 1970s sky with the astronauts strapped inside the space capsule like in a Volkswagen Beetle. The longing for the 70s is nothing other than a longing for the future, for back then it existed, people knew that everything would change, but it doesn't exist any longer now that everything has changed. I think all cultural epochs are characterised by these two modes, the existence of a future and the absence of a future, and the strange thing is that culture seems to strive towards the absence of future, as if that were its highest form, when all longings have been fulfilled, but it isn't, because then longing turns towards the past, or towards something else that has been lost or was never accomplished, as it did in the years prior to the First World War, a war no one expected and no one wanted, driven by forces no one saw, but which with the utmost brutality, first once and then once again, cleared the way for the presence of a new future.

Bonfires

There were few bonfires to be seen where I grew up, except for the burning of dead grass and leaves in early spring and the Midsummer Eve bonfire in summer, nor are there many where I live now. Why this is so I have no idea, for few phenomena can rival fire in beauty – the only thing I can think of is lightning, but lightning is uncontrollable, unlike fire, which can be summoned up anywhere whenever we want, all it takes is a little wood or paper, a matchbox or a lighter, and flame bursts forth. Maybe it has to do with the fact that fires no longer serve a purpose – houses are heated with boilers, and we are rarely so far away from shelter that we need to light a fire to warm ourselves, as people used to do. Nor do we need to burn waste and trash any longer, since it is sorted and recycled instead of being destroyed, and whatever is still burned is combusted in large incinerators in the recycling plants that have replaced landfills. At my maternal grandparents' place, on the other hand, while they were still alive and we went to visit them at their smallholding, which was only about five acres and provided for no more than three cows, a calf and a few hens, there was nearly always a fire burning. It was located between the house and the barn, right below a small mound covered with berry bushes. The ashes were grey and white, strangely smooth and soft to the touch, almost like flour. In some places there were charred remains of wood poking out like shipwrecks on a beach, they were hard yet porous at the edges, one could scrape off layers with one's nails, which one couldn't with unburned wood, and black as night. Occasionally there were tin cans there too, which even if they were discoloured by soot seemed perfectly untouched by the inferno that had destroyed all the other rubbish the tins had arrived with. One of my clearest childhood memories is of this place. The fields are covered by a thin layer of snow, with the brown soil showing through in places, the sky is greyish white, the landscape motionless, the way it sometimes is in winter. My grandfather is standing in front of the fire, dressed in the blue boiler suit he always wore, the brown wellingtons, the black cap with the short brim. He must have just tossed the last load of rubbish on the fire, for he is standing quite still, while the flames, yellow and trembling, stretch up maybe half a metre into the air in front of him, the only movement in this simple image. I suppose I thought of fire as a creature with a separate existence, independent of the material it rose from and fickle in nature, for one moment it might twist and turn, flinging itself fitfully here and there as if enraged or troubled, while the next moment it stood still and erect stretching towards the sky, as if at peace with itself. When I recall this memory now, with the little man standing upright in the unmoving landscape in front of the brightly burning fire, it is time I think of. How time moves at different speeds, as if it consisted of strata, and Granddad, who has been dead for twenty years, existed within one stratum where time tore along, while the spruces on the hill on the other side of the property existed in another slower one, and the hill itself was in one slower still, while the fire, ostensibly the most fleeting of all, since it vanished from the scene later that day, exists within the innermost stratum, where time stands perfectly still and everything is always the same. For that is how fire is, it is always the same, and this timelessness is what we invoke when we light a fire, and what makes it so beautiful and so terrible. In front of the fire we stand before the abyss.

Operation

There was something slightly absent-minded about one of our daughters when she was little, somehow she never quite paid attention. Since she didn't seem unintelligent, I thought it might be due to a hint of dreamy introversion in her character, which in other respects was light-hearted and sociable. But a few months ago they did a hearing test at the public health centre which revealed that her hearing is significantly impaired. So what I had observed wasn't dullness, that's not why she seemed inattentive, it was because she couldn't hear us properly . . . I don't think I have ever felt so guilty about anything. Fortunately it was possible to operate. It turned out that there was a build-up of fluid behind her eardrums and a large polyp in her pharynx, both of which could be removed by relatively uncomplicated procedures. The polyp could be surgically removed, and the fluid could be drained by inserting some tiny tubes into the eardrums. So yesterday I went with her to the hospital. We left early in the morning and sat in the waiting room for a while. She took a picture of our queue number with my phone and of her toy rabbit sitting by itself on the sofa. Before we left home we had put an anaesthetic patch on her wrist, and now she pinched herself from time to time, surprised at how numb her skin felt. Our name was called, and we followed the nurse to a room with two beds separated by a screen, where we had to wait some more. She was told to undress and put on a white smock, while I was handed a garment resembling a raincoat and a plastic cap. Chatting, the nurse removed the patch, then stuck a kind of nozzle into my daughter's arm, explaining it was for the medicine that would make her sleep. Shortly after she left us alone, a boy was wheeled into the room on a bed. From behind the screen we could hear him crying, and a woman trying to comfort him. I looked at my daughter and asked her if she was afraid. She shook her head and pressed the rabbit to her chest. When I grow up I want to be a nurse, she said. It's a fine job, I said. When the nurse came for us half an hour later the boy was asleep, while the woman sat next to him in a chair fiddling with her mobile phone. In the operating theatre the woman who had to be the anaesthesiologist leaned over my daughter and explained to her what she was going to do while she connected a tube to the nozzle in her arm. That she would soon receive a medicine which would make her sleep and that she would feel a faint pressure in her hand, but it wouldn't hurt. She asked if the rabbit was really allowed to be there, and it was, and then she said that she wanted to be a nurse when she grew up. The next moment, as she lay with her head on the pillow gazing up at the lamp above her, both her eyeballs rolled up so that only the whites were visible. It was sinister, as if consciousness had been sucked out of her, like loose parts through a hole in the fuselage of a plane. You can go and wait now, they told me. And take the rabbit with you, so it doesn't get blood on it. She won't notice. I took the rabbit and walked out, then sat in a chair below the window with the stuffed animal on my lap. Not long after, the nurse wheeled her out. She was still under anaesthesia, her eyes were shut, but she was trembling, spasms ran through her, and there were blood spots on her white chest. I had never seen anything so awful. She'll wake up in about half an hour, the nurse said and left the bed next to me. Everything went fine. So I sat there next to the trembling little body for half an hour, whereupon she woke up, just as they had said. She sat up, confused and frightened as if she was doing it in her sleep, and felt about her with her hands. I put the rabbit in front of one of them, and when she felt it there, she pressed it to her breast. How are you doing? I asked. She looked at me and cried. Lie down and rest a little, I said. She did, and fell asleep again. The next time she woke up, she was almost her usual self, just a little fainter and meeker. The nurse brought her an ice cream, which she ate even though she said her stomach hurt. After another half-hour she felt well enough to go home. She was pale and quiet, but she did fine walking down all the corridors, out to the parking lot and over to the car. On the way I stopped at the big toyshop in the old regimental area of Ystad, she was allowed to choose whatever she wanted. We ended up buying a house with a family of plastic rabbits in it. As we stood in line to pay for it she suddenly covered her mouth with her hand, then ran crouching out of the shop. I removed my card from the terminal, put the house in a plastic bag and hurried after her. She was bent double just in front of the car, vomiting on the tarmac. When I reached her it was over. She straightened up. I looked at the vomit. It was dark red. Is that blood? she asked. It looks like it, I said. Is it dangerous? she asked. Oh no, not at all, I said. You probably swallowed it while they were operating. Does it feel better now? Yes, she said. Now I'm fine! As we swung out onto the road, she remembered the time she had been ill and ate blueberry soup, and her vomit was totally blue. Not only that, I said. You threw up all over the white wallpaper. We never got it out, you know. No, she said, laughing. But tell me, I said, why did you run over to the car to vomit? Couldn't you just have been sick on the tarmac right outside the door? I don't know, she said. It felt safer somehow.

Manholes

With their round flat shape, rust-brown colour and various raised patterns and inscriptions, manhole covers look like large coins. That they are found in every city and town, at least in the Western world, shows that they perform their function in the best possible way and have found their ultimate form, for even constructions and inventions obey Darwin's law of the survival of the fittest. Normally I don't notice them, but when I do, for example when the car ahead swerves around a manhole cover and I realise that the driver is superstitious, since it is a common compulsive idea that it brings bad luck to step on or drive over them, I often think that there is something Roman about manholes. The Romans settled upon a certain urban model incorporating their constructions and inventions, which they reproduced in every single town, not merely to leave their mark as vainer civilisations might do – and in some matters the Romans did so too – but quite simply because they proved most practical. I am thinking of the aqueducts, the roads, the city walls, the public baths, the theatres, the circuses, the encampments, the administrative buildings. This view is superficial, and the reasoning is of the very simplest kind: manholes are all alike and are found everywhere, just like certain features of the Roman Empire. But something else happens when manholes are opened. I remember well the first time I witnessed it. It happened on the road right outside the house where I grew up. A car from the municipality was parked by the side of the road when we came home from school. Two men were at work there. The rusty cover was lying on the tarmac next to the manhole, not flat but on top of something, probably to make it easier to get hold of later when they replaced it. I remember that all of us took turns trying to lift the cover, and maybe the reason I remember this is that it was so much heavier than it looked, it wouldn't budge, and that feeling, that something is radically different than expected, is at once exciting and terrible, one wants the world to be predictable, and the tremendous weight of the cover, which was neither very wide nor very thick, was uncanny.

Where the manhole cover had always lain there was now a hole. The hole was dark, maybe two or three metres deep, and there were metal rungs set in the wall. What the two men were doing I no longer know, but I remember that one of them climbed down into the hole and disappeared, and that I caught a glimpse of what was down there. A low narrow passage, more like a tunnel, ran underneath the road. Water was trickling along it.

That was all. That was the secret of the manhole. That its interior was exposed in this way and was no longer a secret should have dispelled the mystery. But it didn't, on the contrary it grew, for there was something fantastical about a passage beneath the road, under the ground, in the middle of the otherwise commonplace world I saw every day from the window when I ate in the kitchen, and which every day we ran around playing in.

I am still drawn to everything below ground. Hospital corridors that stretch for miles, which one goes down into in one place and comes up from in quite another, maybe far from the hospital itself. Abandoned subway tracks. Catacombs. Cave systems in holiday locations. Enormous subterranean defence works from the Cold War, secret bomb shelters in big cities, bunkers. It's not so much the power of the chthonic I am drawn to, I don't think, the strangeness of the underground realm – though it might be tempting to imagine a kind of gravity of the soul, drawing it down towards what it once was and will once again become. No, it's much simpler than that, most of all it probably has to do with the dynamics between the visible and the hidden, between what we know and what we don't know. The more we know about the world the greater the pull of what we don't know, and every tunnel, every grotto, every subterranean chamber is a confirmation of what we have always felt, that nothing ends with what the eyes can see.

Windows

One of the prime functions of houses is to neutralise the weather, to create a place where the wind doesn't sting, rain and snow can't enter and rising and falling temperatures don't apply. Ideally the house temperature should be the same in winter, when it is below zero outside, as in summer, when the temperature rises towards thirty degrees Celsius. This place, which we call 'inside', is therefore engaged in a constant battle against the elements. The walls are thick, so that winds cannot penetrate but instead are forced up over them and guided on their way without touching anything inside, and insulated so that warm air, so desirable in the winter half of the year, does not seep out. Roofs are covered with waterproof materials and slanted so that water everywhere flows down towards the edges, where it is collected in gutters that run around the whole house and lead the water down to the ground through vertical drainpipes, usually one on each corner. The weak points of houses are the windows, which are of a much finer construction than the walls, both because they are thinner and because they are made of a material as fragile as glass, set in wooden frames almost like struts and also considerably thinner than the wood of the walls. Unlike walls, windows can break, which would spell disaster for the house, since wind, rain and cold air would then rush in, and windows also deteriorate faster and might for instance get draughty, letting in cold air. So why put windows in a house when they make the otherwise solid construction fragile and vulnerable? It isn't to regulate the airflow, as one might think when the residents open the windows to let in fresh air because the inside air has grown stale or is saturated with cooking smells, for one could easily have made hatches of the same material and thickness as the surrounding walls. No, the hatches in a house are made of glass so that the residents can look out. This means that 'inside' is not an entirely unambiguous category; if it was, houses might have walls several metres thick made of solid brick with unbroken surfaces, or for that matter might be dug into the ground or built inside excavations in mountains. But an absolute and unambiguous 'inside' is undesirable, despite the advantages it would have with regard to neutralising weather conditions. When we are 'inside', we must at the same time be able to see 'outside'. One might imagine that this is due to a desire for control, that we need to see who is approaching the house in case they have hostile intentions, but that can't be it either, since we cover the windows in the evenings and at night, and just when it is most likely that something hostile might approach under cover of darkness, we make sure that we can't see out. Besides, 'inside' is penetrated by 'outside' in other ways. For instance, it is common to keep plants in the house in mini-habitats, so-called flower pots, which seek to simulate the 'outside' as much as possible so that the plants may grow and thrive even in the plant-hostile indoor environment. But this occurs under highly controlled conditions, it is as if the flowers' 'outside' is provided with an 'inside' of its own within the greater 'inside', except inversely, for in a flower pot the 'outside', that is the water and the soil, is kept 'inside' by the walls of the pot. No one grows flowers or vegetables indoors without these extra walls, for example in mounds of soil on the floor; quite the contrary, all soil, pebbles, sand, blades of grass, pine needles and leaves which for some reason end up indoors are unwanted and removed immediately. The same principle applies to water. If water is spilled on the floor or on the table, that is in the free form in which water exists outside, it is wiped up at once. Water is only allowed indoors in containers or pipes, and therefore also has its own 'inside' within the 'inside' of the house. This is so because water and soil, plants and leaves all possess forces and dynamics of the outer world that even in small quantities destroy the 'inside', which is characterised by the opposite, namely the static and the unchanging. A little moisture on the wall and it gets mouldy, rots, disintegrates. Then the wind blows through it, more moisture enters, and finally, if this is allowed to continue, the house will collapse, its organic elements will turn to soil, which plants and trees will root themselves in and grow out of, so that the mineral elements of the house too will eventually disappear, into the forest, down into the ground. When despite this we don't wall ourselves up in indoor environments so impenetrable that everything external is kept 'outside', even out of view, it is because we ourselves belong 'outside', for not only does the outside keep us alive, with its water and its earthbound plants, but we ourselves are made of water, we too are earthbound, and our striving towards the static, the unchanging and the neutral is a denial of this, as we all know and feel deep down inside, so that the opening provided by the windows, which is turned not only towards the 'outside' but also towards the 'outside' 'inside' ourselves, is an existential entity that we can't live without. How ambivalent we are in relation to these categories of 'inside' and 'outside' becomes apparent if we consider the coffin, which by virtue of being our final dwelling, our last defence against the elements, our final 'inside', in large measure denies our true nature, but not entirely: in that case, the coffin too would have windows.